Taoism for Beginners

Understand & Apply Core Taoist Principles & Practices

By: Jane Rivers

Copyright © 2020 by Jane Rivers

ALL RIGHTS RESERVED

No part of this book may be reproduced, stored in a retrieval system, or transmitted in any form or by any means, electronic, mechanical, photocopying, recording, scanning, or otherwise, without the prior written permission of the publisher.

Limit of Liability/Disclaimer of Warranty: the publisher and the author make no representations or warranties with respect to the accuracy or completeness of the contents of this work and specifically disclaim all warranties, including without limitation warranties of fitness for a particular purpose. No warranty may be created or extended by sales or promotional materials. The advice and strategies contained herein may not be suitable for every situation. This work is sold with the understanding that the publisher is not engaged in rendering medical, legal or other professional advice or services. If professional assistance is required, the services of a competent professional person should be sought. Neither the publisher nor the author shall be liable for damages arising herefrom. The fact that an individual, organization or website is referred to in this work as a citation and/or potential source of further information does not mean that the author or the publisher endorses the information the individuals, organization or website may provide or recommendations they/it may make. Further, readers should be aware that websites listed on this work may have changed or disappeared between when this work was written and when it is read.

Table of contents

Introduction 1
Chapter 1: Understanding the Way 3
Chapter 2: The Key Core Principles of Taoism 21
Chapter 3: Taoism for Beginners 38
Chapter 4: Advanced Actions to Accentuate Your Practices 59
Chapter 5: The Way of Internals for a Healthful Body 81
Chapter 6: The Taoism Diet for Energy & Longevity 102
Chapter 7: Combining Spiritualism as a Daily Practice 126
Chapter 8: Putting Taoism into Practice in Your Daily Life ... 156
References: 166

Introduction

Understanding the way or the Tao (also pronounced "Dao") is really a matter of journeying through the core of oneself as an inner perception of beingness. This occurs while also recognising the need to follow through with actioning that allows for the flow of "The Way." This idea may sound tricky, however, as you become more and more familiar with the principles and the practices steeped in historical and ancient culture, you'll certainly enjoy the spiritual experience which allows this infamous flow. So, let that be our first understanding of the Tao, that we are mostly being and allowing, even though there are some added applications that we'll be incorporating, too.

You might not be aware that Taoism is a major world religion that started long ago in China. And many believe that it started in the 6th century B.C. with a philosopher who was named at birth, Lao Tzu. He wrote down all of his subsequent teachings in a famous book called the Tao Te Ching, but no one truly knows whether Lao Tzu was real or not.

Legends also propose that Lao Tzu became disillusioned with all of the war, corruption, and violence in China, so he decided to leave it behind him. It is said that on his way out of China, a guard would not let the old man go until Lao Tzu wrote down all of his teachings. This is how Lao Tzu wrote down the Tao Te Ching, which is now the most revered and sacred book of Taoism. Then, according to legend, he rode away on a water buffalo, and no one ever saw him again.

It is clear that Lao Tzu never intended to create any type of new religion. He didn't seem to want to be a leader or a prophet, however, the people of China loved his teachings and his way of understanding through his wisdom. And soon, all of his written ideas became combined with the ancient customs of Chinese folk religions, too. This is why Taoism began to include beliefs in such deities as gods, goddesses, magicians, and even dragons. The common people also added spells and charms, as well as the worship of their ancestors.

Welcome to the book. It is my hope that you will gain a thorough understanding of the beauty and mysticism of Taoism through its history, practices, and its applications which have been enjoyed, practiced, and studied for centuries.

Chapter 1: Understanding the Way

The History of 'The Way'

Taoism (also known as Daoism) is the world-renowned Chinese philosophy attributed to the famous teachings of Lao Tzu (c. 500 BCE) who contributed to the folk religion of the people of that era. These commoners were primarily located within the rural areas of China, and so it became the official religion of the country. This occurred during the Tang Dynasty. Taoism is known as a religion and a philosophy, and both of these references are considered to be correct adjectives for the name.

Taoism is regarded as the oldest of China's three religion-philosophies, with Buddhism and Confucianism being the other two which are practiced in modern China, even today.

Like Confucianism, Taoism emerged during what is known as the Age of Philosophers and is said to have been founded by a very humble, Chinese mystic named Lao Tzu. Many influential Taoist scholars such as the Taoist master Zhuangzi (or Chuang Tzu) are also said to have made contributions to it over time. Some historians have acknowledged that Taoism is really a revival of religious thought which was most dominant in the Shang Dynasty occurring from 1558 to 1102 B.C.

As we already know, Taoism has both a philosophical and a religious tradition in Chinese history. And as philosophical Taoism flourished early in the 5th century B.C., however, Taoism as a religious center did not develop until the 1st century A.D. In addition to Confucianism, it ranks as the second major belief system in traditional Chinese thought. In fact, the vastness of the philosophy of Taoism is outlined in the world-famous Tao Te Ching, offering a practical way of life. Also known by many as "The Way."

Scholars on Taoism

It's interesting to hear from scholars regarding Taoism, too. Dr. Robert Eno from Indiana University said "When we speak of 'Daoism' in the Classical period, we generally mean by the term the ideas of two rather mysterious texts that date from the Warring States era. They are the 'Dao de jing' (Classic of the Way and of Virtue) by Laozi, and the works of the quirky recluse Zhuangzi, which appear in a book that takes his name as its title. Daoism appears to have begun as an escapist movement during the early Warring States period, and in some ways, it makes sense to see it as an outgrowth of Confucianism and its doctrine of 'timeliness.'

That doctrine originated with Confucius's motto: 'When the Way (dao) prevails in the world, appear; when it does not, hide!'"

Dr. Eno continued: "Daoism appears to have begun as an escapist movement during the chaotic late Zhou, and in some ways it makes sense to see it as an outgrowth of Confucianism, which had preached a special doctrine called 'timeliness,' that rationalized the urge to withdraw from the troubled society of the age."

He went on to write "Confucianism ultimately became the most influential school of thought in China, and its basic ideas, much altered by the interpretations of later scholars and power holders, became the core of China's official 'state ideology.' Throughout the Imperial period of China, beginning with the 2nd century B.C. and ending only in 1905, generation after generation of young and ambitious men competed for jobs and recognition by taking state-wide examinations that tested their grasp of Confucian principles."

Dr. Eno concluded that "Although Confucianism seemed to prevail as state ideology, its down-to-earth teachings, rather rigid ideas, and relentlessly idealistic moral goods often strained the patience of the very people who most endorsed Confucian points of view. In time, another intellectual tradition born during the chaos of the late Zhou Dynasty, Daoism, came to be highly influential as a type of counterbalance to Confucianism. The mainstream intellectual tradition of China's educated elite may sometimes be pictured as a confluence of Confucian and Daoist tributaries. For this reason, it is important to explore the ideas of the original Daoist texts. There is another reason: they're more fun."

Birgitta Augustin of New York University stated this in her writing: "Indigenous to China, Daoism arose as a secular school of thought with a strong metaphysical foundation around 500 B.C., during a time when fundamental spiritual ideas were emerging in both the East and the West. Two core texts form the basis of Daoism: the Laozi and the Zhuangzi, attributed to the two eponymous masters, whose historical identity, like the circumstances surrounding the compilation of their texts, remains uncertain. The Laozi—also called the Daodejing, or Scripture of the Way and Virtue—has been understood as a set of instructions for virtuous rulership or for self-cultivation. It stresses the concept of nonaction or noninterference with the natural order of things. Dao, usually translated as the Way, may be understood as the path to achieving a state of enlightenment resulting in longevity or even immortality. But Dao, as something ineffable, shapeless, and conceived of as an infinite void, may also be understood as the unfathomable origin of the world and as the progenitor of the dualistic forces, yin and yang. Yin, associated with shade, water, west, and the tiger, and yang, associated with light, fire, east, and the dragon, are the two alternating phases of cosmic energy; their dynamic balance brings cosmic harmony."

Augustin also wrote: "Over time, Daoism developed into an organized religion—largely in response to the institutional structure of Buddhism—with an ever-growing canon of texts and pantheon of gods, and a significant number of schools with often distinctly different ideas and approaches. At times, some of these schools were also politically active. Along with Buddhism, Daoism today is one of the two dominant religions in the Chinese-speaking world. Although the attainment of immortality appears to be a rather esoteric and challenging objective, Daoism, with its popular and cultic elements, continues to provide practical guidance through codes of behavior and physical regimens, as well as talismans and ritual services that help regulate the everyday life of its many followers..."

She continued in her writing to say: "By the 12th century, Daoism, Confucianism, and Buddhism—known as the three doctrines—were seen as mutually complementary, although at times they competed for influence at court. Indeed, from that time forward, the pantheons of these doctrines often overlapped, and their rituals, architecture, and art appeared similar, often as a consequence of commissioning the same artisans to create images and edifices."

As we can see from the scholars' acknowledgement and study, Taoism caught on very quickly in the country of China. One of the major reasons was because it told its followers how they could reach 'heaven' and it also explained man's place within the enormity of the universe. Eventually too, duties presided over by shaman were taken over by Taoist priests and Taoism merged with popular folklore and belief systems, becoming associated with beliefs in ghosts, exorcism, demons, faith healing, magic, and even with fortune telling.

Eventually Taoism moved away from many of the original teachings of Lao Tzu. And this occurred because of the addition of an elaborate array of gods and rituals. Some Taoist ideas were incorporated into Confucianism and Chinese Buddhism too, but a lot of Buddhists and Confucianists accused Taoists of practicing occultism and/or witchcraft.

During the Han dynasty which occurred from 202 B.C. to A.D. 220, there were an array of state sacrifices which were made in Lao Tzu's honor, and so Taoism developed as a so-called "philosophy of spontaneity and naturalism" which was also thoroughly highlighted through its rituals and techniques for achieving immortality as a main pursuit. Taoism spread throughout China and became firmly established during what is known as "The Six Dynasties Period" (occurring from 220-588 A.D.) At this time, many Taoist temples and abbeys were highlighted throughout the expanse of the vast Chinese countryside.

Taoism was exceptionally popular too, while Confucianism was mainly practiced by the upper classes within China during The Six Dynasties Period. Taoism won many away from Confucianism, and this was said to be because Confucianism did not promise any ascertainment relating to immortality, nor did it answer the posed questions of the cosmos like Taoism could. Immortality was something high on the list for many people of that time.

The Later History of Taoism

Taoism was also somewhat threatened by its competition from Buddhism, beginning around the A.D. 3rd century. And so, Taoism as a religion (and a revered philosophy) underwent a reformed movement in which it became more organized. At this period of time, some of its most outlandish beliefs and rituals were muted and lessened. Moral conduct was something which was inadvertently pushed as the primary means of obtaining immortality. And those who practiced esoteric rituals and diets were encouraged to do so in secret. At this time, Buddha was declared a Taoist saint, an unlikely but hugely popular theme of the time. Additionally, the addition of crude rituals and esoteric beliefs persisted though, even despite the best efforts to reduce their necessity.

Lao Tzu (also known as Lao-tze)

Lao Tzu (604 to 517 B.C.) is still regarded by some as the founder of the Taoism philosophy. No one truly knows whether he was an actual person, though. And it is only via his Tao Te Ching which was left behind that there is any evidence of a man at all, in truth. Many people think he was real and have a thorough admiration for his intelligence and knowing which comes about from his teachings.

There are records of a Lao-tze who lived in the central part of China, working as an astrologer and as a librarian for a Zhou dynasty emperor at the same time period. This Lao-tze was reported to have met with Confucius and called him "...egotistical and overly proud." Lao-tze is said to be the second-most-widely-read poet in the world, even today, and after that of the world-famous Shakespeare.

The name Lao-tze means "grand old master" or "old philosopher" in the Chinese language. Many wise attributions like, "A journey of a thousand miles begins with a single step" have been lovingly attributed to him, too. It's also true that paintings of Lao-tze usually depict the legendary human as an old man who has long white hair and a straight (and long) white beard, sometimes portrayed riding a water buffalo or an ox, and also being seen with a scroll in his right hand.

Lao-tze was a philosopher of politics and war, and similar to that of Confucius, he lived at a time when war and political chaos were part and parcel of normal life. He argued that politics was about ruling, and that if the social rule became too tyrannical, the domestic order plunged into chaos as a result of that greedy effort. He also noted, that on the other hand, order could start falling apart with minimal stress, so the wisest ruler might intervene as soon as he could see this appearing within the kingdom. He additionally went on to say that a wise ruler does not wait. He must act immediately.

One particular warfare, he argued, was that spirituality was of far greater importance than the strategic interpretation of yielding to greater force to find the right moment to strike. Additionally, he also concluded that the strategic idea is verily important; that there is not one weapon or one technology to win all battles. His belief relied on the onus that a ruler should always adapt one's army to the circumstances at hand, including the weather, and the terrain of battle that was being impeded upon the current battleground.

Early Taoist Thinkers and Schools of Thought

Taoism formally grew from religious ideas that were circulated at the academy of Chi-gate. And this increased activity grew in the 4th century B.C.

Among the earliest thinkers that were active at the time was Tsou Yen, a gentleman regarded as the creator of the Chinese and more 'scientific' view of the universe based on the basis of yin and yang. Also noteworthy were Sung Hsing, Yin Wen and Yang Chu, who pushed for a philosophy which began to revolve around individualism related to salvation. There was also a gentleman named Mozi, and he was the leader of the Mohism 'Universal Love' school. Another gentleman called Yang Chu, was so committed to living as long as possible and avoiding trouble that he would not even "...pluck out a single hair even if it might have benefitted the whole world."

Yang Chu was particularly influential within this time period of the 4th century B.C. He drew on ancient physical theories, and primarily the idea of chi (qi, or breath) which was regarded as the "breath of all life." His main plight was to collect all the finer parts which were associated with chi. This was primarily for the innate purposes of prolonging one's life, and to additionally find happiness as well as elevated spirituality within the practice of Taoism. A number of methods were added too, including the importance of the believer's diet and in consuming certain herbs, which were duly developed to accumulate these finer parts of chi.

Still in 4th century B.C., the newly formed School of Lao-tze and Zhuangzi (Chuang Tzu, 369-280 B.C.) were exploring similar ideas to Yang Chu. The many scholars there developed the theory of Tao, that is to say:

1. That the fundamental basis of all beings is based on a state of non-being rather than being, and
2. that it was possible to avoid death through uniting oneself with the universal nothingness of Tao; and
3. the best way to do this was to empty oneself of desires and live like a hermit.

These fascinating belief systems as incorporations were loved and celebrated by the people. And so, Taoism became ever popular in 4th century B.C. within China.

The Similarity of 'The Way' in Confucianism

Dr. Eno went onto write: "Even in the Confucian 'Analects,' we see signs of a Confucian trend towards absolute withdrawal. The character and comportment of Confucius's best disciple, Yan Yuan, who lived in obscurity in an impoverished lane yet 'did not alter his joy,' suggest this early tendency towards eremitism (the "hermit" lifestyle).

In Book 18 of the 'Analects,' Confucius seems half drawn to the path of absolute social withdrawal, too: In Chu there was a madman known as the Carriage Greeter who passed before the carriage of Confucius singing, 'Phoenix! Phoenix! How your virtue has declined! Don't preach about what is past; don't race after what is yet to come. Be done! Be done! In this age, entanglements of state are perilous!' Confucius climbed down wishing to speak with him, but the Carriage Greeter darted off. (Analects 18.5)

The comparison to Confucianism is clear and is noted by Dr. Eno within his writings.

From Analects 18.6:

Chang Ju and Jie Ni were plowing the fields in harness together. Confucius passed by and sent Zilu over to ask directions. "Who's that holding the carriage reins?" asked Chang Ju.

"That is Kong Qiu," replied Zilu.

"Kong Qiu of Lu?"

"Yes!" said Zilu.

"Why, then," said Chang Ju, "he knows where he can go!"

Zilu then asked Jie Ni.

"And who are you?" asked Jie Ni.

"I am Zhong You," replied Zilu.

"Are you the Zhong You who is a disciple of Kong Qiu of Lu?"

"I am," said Zilu.

Jie Ni said "The world is inundated now. Who can change it? Would you not be better off joining those who have fled from the world altogether, instead of following someone who flees from this man to that one?"

Then the two of them went on with their plowing. Zilu returned to report to Confucius.

The Master's brow furrowed. "I cannot flock together with the birds and beasts!" he cried. "If I am not a fellow traveler with men such as these, then with whom? If only the Way prevailed in the world, I would not have to try to change it!"

Dr. Eno penned that: "Righteous hermits were much admired in Classical China, and men who withdrew from society to live in poverty 'in the cliffs and caves' paradoxically often enjoyed a type of celebrity status. The legend of Bo Yi and Shu Qi, the hermits who descended from their mountain retreat because of the righteousness of King Wen of Zhou, led to the popular idea of hermits as virtue-barometers – they rose to the mountains when power was in the hands of immoral rulers, but would come back down to society when a sage king finally appeared. Patrician lords very much valued visits from men with reputations as righteous hermits, and this probably created the opportunity for men to appear at court seeking patronage on the basis of their eremitic purity."

Dr. Eno went on to say that: "Possibly during the 4th century B.C., this eremitic tradition seems to have generated a complex of new ideas that included appreciation for the majestic rhythms of the natural world apart from human society, a celebration of the isolated individual whose lonely stance signalled a unique power of enlightenment, and a growing interest in the potential social and political leverage that such renunciation of social and political entanglements seemed to promise. The product that emerged from these trends is the 'Dao de jing,' perhaps the most famous of all Chinese books."

Zhuangzi (or Master Zhuang's) Influence on Taoism

Zhuangzi (Chuang-tzu, Master Zhuang) was a late 4th century B.C. philosopher and is the pivotal and notable standout in what is known as Classical Philosophical Taoism.

According to the Stanford Encyclopedia of Philosophy, this title states that: "The Zhuangzi is a compilation of his and others' writings at the pinnacle of the philosophically subtle Classical period in China (5th–3rd century B.C.). The period was marked by humanist and naturalist reflections on normativity shaped by the metaphor of a dào—a social or a natural path. Traditional orthodoxy understood Zhuangzi as an anti-rational, credulous, follower of a mystical Laozi. Centuries later, elements of Zhuangzi's naturalism, helped shape Chan Buddhism (Japanese Zen)—a distinctively Chinese, naturalist blend of Daoism and Buddhism with its emphasis on focused engagement in our everyday ways of life."

As we focus upon the scholars and credible sources of information given with regard to the study of Taoism, we begin to understand how Taoism (also known as "The Way") was formed. We can see that these writings and teachings began to take their hold through the period of time when Taoism grew throughout China, in line with Confucianism and Buddhism, but also as a separate source to those, but with some similarities, too. Its growth and mechanism of action had many instigators (including philosophers, Masters, gentlemen, and spiritualists) who had an impact on its cause and effect throughout the scope of The Six Dynasties Period (occurring from 220-588 A.D.)

Christine Gross-Loh wrote about Zhuangzi in The Atlantic in October, 2013, and stated that Zhuangzi "…taught that we should train ourselves to become 'spontaneous' through daily living, rather than closing ourselves off through what we think of as rational decision-making. In the same way that one deliberately practices the piano in order to eventually play it effortlessly, through our everyday activities we train ourselves to become more open to experiences and phenomena so that eventually the right responses and decisions come spontaneously, without angst, from the heart-mind."

Additionally, Chow Chung-yan wrote in The South China Morning Post in December 2012, and noted that "While Confucius emphasises social virtues, harmonious order and hierarchy, Zhuangzi's works are far more existential and transcendental. His thinking is individual rather than collective, and his poetic writings have inspired generations of writers. In many ways, Zhuangzi is an artist philosopher in the same vein as Friedrich Nietzsche, deemed eccentric by the mainstream but loved by writers and artists. For millennia, Confucius was an honoured and revered sage, his teachings publicly embraced by emperors - who might not necessarily believe in them. Many rulers read Laozi for his ideas on the subtle interplay of opposite forces, although few would endorse his teachings in public. Zhuangzi's stress on individualism and transcendental freedom, however, made him a spiritual haven for intellectuals looking to escape omnipresent collectivism."

Zhuangzi famously wrote that "Where there is impossibility, there is possibility; and where there is possibility, there is impossibility. It is because there is right, that there is wrong; it is because there is wrong, there is right. Thereupon the self is also the other; the other is also the self."

In essence, the patterning shown here in this wisdom (and via the understanding written about within newspapers and texts) is: that there is duality within the understanding and practice within Taoism, whether this is as a religious practice or as a philosophical belief system, or both. Additionally, it is important to understand that when we are able to recognize opposites or dualities, then this allows us to be at peace with the understandings of "The Way." And, in essence, it teaches us to have more acceptance and flow, whether or not we are in agreement with our circumstances, ways of perception, or attitudes, or not. Here, we can understand that we too, as individuals, are made up of many parts, and some of those parts are the shadow (or negative polarity) aspects of us, as well as what might be considered to be the light, or the good within us. And in Taoism, the judgment is invalid anyway. Although, that is not to say that we cannot think about things as being right or wrong, light and dark, etc.

Taoism & Confucianism; The Han Dynasty Time Period (221-206 B.C.)

Dr. Eno also wrote down that "The early Han emperors were careful to maintain the structure of religious symbolism that the First Emperor of the Qin had constructed to convey the exalted status of the emperor. Complex rituals of sacrifice and the maintenance of a widespread system of shrines, sustained by imperial funds, were characteristics of state religion that the Former Han emperors took most seriously. During the reign of Wen-di, considerable effort was expended on such shrines. But apart from these activities, the first Han emperors did not emulate the Qin example of designating a specific school of thought to represent state orthodoxy."

He also noted that: "During Wen-di's time, two sharply contrasting ideological tendencies developed at court. The first of these owed a great deal to Wen-di's principal consort, the Empress Dou (another formidable female figure in early Han politics). Empress Dou was devoted to the texts of Daoism. We are not quite sure what the term 'Daoism' denoted at this time, but it is recorded that among the texts she most treasured was the 'Dao de jing.' The empress sponsored Daoism strongly at court, and insisted that her eldest son, the future emperor, study it. In the form that Daoism took at this time, the ideology was generally referred to as the 'Huang-Lao School,' with the word Huang denoting the name of the Yellow Emperor, who was bracketed with Laozi. Twenty years ago, archaeologists excavated from an early Han grave a set of texts that included among them the 'Dao de jing.' Others of the texts spun doctrines around the figure of the Yellow Emperor, and we now presume that the full corpus of texts such as these comprised the basis of Huang-Lao ideology.

Eno's words also highlighted that "Huang-Lao ideology seems to have advocated an extreme form of laissez-faire administration, in combination with a regular pattern of government actions or regulations that was conceived as harmonizing with the rhythms of nature. This minimalist program dominated Wen-di's court and that of his son, Jing-di, who was under the sway of his mother. Huang-Lao combined in certain ways with Legalism, a relationship we saw earlier in the doctrines of the 'Han Feizi,' and it is recorded that the ministers who rose to power during the reigns of Wen-di and Jing-di were generally Huang-Lao or Legalist adepts..

But Wen-di also was the first Han emperor to patronize Confucian studies. During the reign of Wen-di, Confucian membership among the Erudites increased, and included men selected for their mastery of certain texts that Confucianism had come to hold most sacred, known as 'classics.' Some of these Confucian 'classics' had become extremely difficult to obtain because of the prohibition on them that had been in force between 213 and 191 B.C. Wen-di endorsed vigorous efforts to recover these lost texts and even sent one of his highest ministers to travel to Shandong to recover the 'Book of Documents' from the memory of an aged Confucian scholar. We will discuss further the rise of Confucianism during the early Han in a separate section...

In sum, during the reign of Wen-di, forms of Daoism and Confucianism both thrived at court. Between the two, Daoism was clearly in the dominant position, and would become even more so during the two decades following Wen-di's death. However, as some thinker once said, 'Reversal is the motion of the Dao' – the Dao will bring down the mighty and raise the lowly. This was to be the case with Daoism and Confucianism at the Han court."

The idea that the Tao was a force all unto itself is clear in Dr. Eno's practical writings. He suggests that The Way is all encompassing despite the methodologies of those using or not using it. Put simply, Th Way is competent by itself, whether or not it is being utilized or changed, compared to, or implemented or negated. It just is.

The Rebirth of Taoism in Modern Culture

The religion and/or philosophy of Taoism was banned by the Communists in the year of 1949. Under Communist rule, many Taoist temples were completely ransacked and the persecution which ensued also reduced the number of practicing Taoists to almost none. Temples were then utilized as government offices, schools, and dormitories, too.

It is truly difficult to gauge the number of practicing Taoist in today's modern world, and this is because Taoism is a personalized religion and philosophy that does not require attendance to formalized meetings or temples, at all. At true Taoist temples, tourists and fortune seekers often outnumber devout Taoists by a big margin.

Journalist, Ian Johnson wrote a segment in 2011, in the New York Review of Books, and he stated that "During the Mao years many of Daoism's traditions, such as fortune telling, geomancy, possession by spirits, and popular rituals, were banned as superstitious. But it's been making a limited comeback. Although still dwarfed by Buddhism, as well as newer religions, like Christianity, the number of Daoist temples has at least tripled over the past fifteen years, according to official figures. Priests and nuns who run the temples provide services to pilgrims and go out into the community to consecrate homes or businesses and perform funerals. Others spread Daoist ideas through martial arts, such as Tai Chi, or medicine---two disciplines rooted in Daoism."

Taoism's Uneasy Existence with the Chinese Communist Government

Ian Johnson wrote a segment in 2013 in the New York Review of Books, "Back in the 1980s and 1990s, government officials widely saw Daoism as the most 'backward religion' practices like palm reading or fengshui were routinely condemned as 'feudal superstition.' But faced with the rising popularity of foreign religions, especially Christianity, the government is beginning to endorse Daoism, too."

Ian Johnson wrote a segment in 2011, in the New York Review of Books, "The Daodejing, says a lot about ruling, and one translation of that work's title is 'The Way and its Power.' Certainly, the text can be read profitably by authoritarians; (translations from Lao-tzu's Taoteching, Copper Canyon Press, 2009): the rule of the sage empties the mind but fills the belly/ Then again there are other verses that might well trouble a government trying to fight a perception that it is corrupt:/ The reason people are hungry is that those above levy so many taxes / or: the reason people are hard to rule is that those above are so forceful."

Another part of Taoism that isn't so easy for the government to swallow is that it has actually become a world religion, one that cannot be controlled very easily. In truth, the vast explosion of popular interest into Taoism and Chinese religion cannot be muted, despite what government authorities may try to do.

Sometimes, the more China's leaders try to use religion for their own purposes, the more difficult it may be to have an actual effect on perceived problems like society's moral decline. Despite the new building of temples, religious life is still very tightly watched over. Many practitioners do find a deeper moral answer in the teachings of Taoism and other religions. Some volunteers at Taoist temples provide food for the poor or engage in relief if disaster strikes. The teachings of compassion and unity with nature also make a valuable contribution in a country where pursued economic gain at the expense of charity has been commonplace over the centuries, and where concern for the environment might have also been overlooked because capitalism has seemed far more important overall.

Chapter 2: The Key Core Principles of Taoism

The Choice of Spiritualism

Many spiritual endeavors are merely emotional or psychological. And in general, religious rituals are defined as worship, but in true honesty, they are either emotional demands or psychological needs which have prevailed since ancient times and are usually steeped in traditional necessity.

Another category of spiritual endeavor might be a result of your own personal spiritual effort and development; one which is not socially supported at all. In essence, working for your personal spiritual development does not come from someone else's charity or kindness. It's a totally personal endeavor that an individual chooses to do with devoted actioning. Cutting through the issues of the emotions, including the inner psychology, mental conceptions or perceptions, as well as personal life problems, provides the necessary progression which can help restore your personal balance and poise as a spiritual being.

In human everyday life, all of us are said to have three spheres. These are the physical, the mental, and the spiritual parts of us. It can't really be denied that all life needs material support, and our entire life is not limited to the material sphere only. Our spirit (or soul) also needs proper development and reflection, though. The direction of human society has changed radically from the pursuit of the spirit to the pursuit of the material world, or how much we 'have' in terms of financial gain and/or resources.

In today's modern world, the material and mental aspects of life are overemphasized and run from the perception of ego and logic, especially in the form of intellectual knowledge which makes some individuals begin to deny the existence of a spiritual level of life, or the need for soul growth at all.

The Need for Spiritual Growth

People need spiritual growth and development to be whole, but they might assert a 'tunnel vision' view of life as the result of advances in scientific research and industrial technology. It's true too, that these aspects do not cover the whole scope of human existence as three-part, triune beings. We cannot use the same methods that apply to material discoveries to explore the spiritual sphere, and it would be difficult to do so, for certain. And so, many become disappointed and deny the existence of a spiritual realm at all. These people never really see the error of using the wrong 'tools,' and thus, they move far from the wholeness of life which can incorporate the spirit as a part of one's individualism.

What we call the 'journey' or the 'spiritual path' is really just the common learnings or teachings of basic life. It's also true that modern education mostly pushes aptitude and living on the physical and mental levels, therefore avoiding spiritual matters on the whole. This way of living doesn't support spiritual development at all, neglecting what some might say is the most essential part of life.

Enhancing Spiritual Development is a Core Need

Spiritual development must be there to deepen and explore the truth in order for a person to achieve the goal of wholeness and balance, which is done step by step. It takes years for most individuals, and it truly depends on how the person receives their spiritual education and works on himself or herself. This is the beginning of individual spiritual development. It's also true that it's a personal matter and so, going 'within' is part and parcel to finding answers.

For true self-cultivation, we could say that the body, mind, and spirit should be equally valued and worked upon. Gaining spiritual achievement develops from physical essence, with the mind as the major link between the physical and the spiritual spheres. Its duty is to organize a harmonious state of enjoyment through a beautiful life. The potential here is everchanging too, and if balance is broken then the scales can be tipped, metaphorically speaking.

In everyday life, very few people are murderers or use violence per say, but many people are emotionally violent. It's very true that many people lose their tempers when things don't go their way. And here, the loss of spiritual qualities as virtues, like patience and tolerance (as examples), can make individuals take a violent emotional path. In fact, it is the mind (or ego) response to things, rather than a more balanced or heart centered approach.

When you are in an eventful circumstance and your mind is not bothered, this is called true peace and true calmness. This occurs when the mind is no longer controlled by circumstances, and therefore, it is free. The freedom of the mind is a powerful, purposeful mind. A very useful mind, indeed. This is truly the key to going further to the source of it via spirituality. And it is important to note that this peace and calm is attained by your own methodical cultivation. Additionally, when the mind is kept on the 'right channel,' then the nature of spiritual essence can be reached and can be seen by way of peacefulness and calmness.

The 7 Stages of the Tao

Stage 1: This occurs when the mind reaches peace and can more easily respond to the subtle and ordinary parts of one's life. It is then easy to discern what worldly things are heavier and that they might be disturbing to your true inner peace. Knowing this can prevent the cause of a downfall.

Stage 2: This stage is when old physical problems clear up by themselves and you don't need to go to physicians any longer. Your physical body and the mind will feel lighter and happier, too.

Stage 3: At this stage, your vitality is regenerated, and you come back to a state that's more natural and begets a healthier life overall. You'll also begin to follow the right way of living as is guided by your growing of wisdom from within.

Stage 4: Stage 4 occurs after you have achieved the foundation of the first stages already mentioned. You can live from your heart space (as opposed to the mind/ego) and not be subject to the lower influences that might be more negative, or ego based. You can now connect with the spiritual realm at this stage.

Stage 5: This stage occurs when an individual refines one's physical energy to be higher, with what might be called essential energy. Through perseverance and cultivation, the physical energy is transformed to become chi.

Stage 6: This later stage comes after transforming the gross chi into more subtle chi. After this, you can begin to transform your chi to be more essential, to live as a spiritual being. Spiritual beings can be in the world and remain subtle or not, just as they so wish to be. They are true spirits who have purpose-filled or spiritually guided lives.

Stage 7: This stage is when the spirit (or soul) is refined and unites completely with the Tao. And now, the ultimate beingness is achieved. This is a true divine path. The individual's light will always respond to lighten the darkness within the world around it, too.

The seven stages to become one with Tao, or to enjoy complete fulfillment, are universal. Any individual who seeks such self-cultivation without seeing any of these positive results will not achieve Tao.

Tao, or the spirit of youth, is untouched and cannot be bent to any personal will or ambition towards greed or gain in the material world. It never fails and never declines, either. To understand this further, it is important to study the Tao Te Ching, which imparts great knowledge about Tao from the key writer known historically as Lao Tzu.

It is also relevant here to know that the initial spirit (your soul) is always in progression and that it's always developing furthermore. It constantly provides the possibility for an entirely new range of life experiences to unfold for each individual, in fact. This is the true essence of universal nature. It does not hold to any past images, nor does it value the common-sense sayings of refined ancient sages. It is a great path discovered by great humans who transcend as human beings. As a self-cultivation methodology, it refreshes one's spirit, mind, and body, and offers fullness and harmony from within.

It is also fundamentally important that individuals attain emotional independence to achieve Tao. It doesn't mean that an individual avoids all emotional relationships, or that you must live absolutely alone. It means that you remain independent to the causations and affects that relationships bring with them.

In truth, spiritual independence is a life pursuit without any guarantee of attaining enlightenment or discovering ultimate truth. An individual who achieves spiritual independence must first achieve emotional independence as a precursor of maintenance and foundation.

An individual's mind is an instrument to unite the spirit (soul) with the physical body. The original origin of the soul is formless. It is made of nothing, but from this nothingness, everything is brought to fruition. This nothingness of the universe is made up of both creative and constructive energy. If you keep your mind in this nothingness, you can profoundly and miraculously imitate the entire process of the universe. Bringing life to you, while allowing, without force or struggle.

The core of the integral spiritual realm of an individual or of the entire universe is an inexpressible, indescribable stillness. However, it has a subtle, inexhaustible movement which can be traced by following the harmonious, gentle pulsations of the integral spiritual realm within its clarity and distinction.

Understanding the Spiritual Origin and Tradition of Taoism

The beings of integrity (Integral Beings) are known as spiritual immortals. These subtle beings are said to exist in realms that are transcendent to time and space. They were the first beings who came from the pure, creative energy of the

Subtle Origin of the universe, and are said to have existed long before the creation of Heaven and Earth.

The Integral Beings are said to have continuously exerted a subtler influence, not only on the whole of mankind and earthly events, but also on the events of the whole universe. Since the dawn of time, everything is constantly changing under the universal law of transformation. Only the Integral Beings are said to be beyond degeneration, and this is because of their continuous and miraculous renewal through self-mastery.

At the dawn of time, the Earth was uninhabited by any beings. The original beings from what is known as the Subtle Origin of the universe combined themselves with the yin, or physical energy of the Earth. This birthed mankind. They are said to be the true ancestors of the entire human race, in fact.

The first inhabitants of Earth were faithful to their divine natures, so they had no need to cultivate or discipline themselves at all. They were contented and enjoyed full, effective lives, without the need to use intellectual functioning at all. Because their energy was so pure and ultimately complete, they did not require any change or self-refinement. They lived exceptionally long and abundant lives. However, after many generations of humans, mankind began to degenerate their thought processes and their ways of living became impure. And so, their subtle, divine energy gradually dissipated, becoming less and less pure over time. It became necessary for human beings to develop their intellectual natures to compensate for the loss of their ability to respond spontaneously and miraculously to the environment around them.

Mankind has the divine essence inside, stemming from the Subtle Origin, but during the course of history, its divinity was covered over by many layers of mental creations, acquisitions, and much confusion, too. Originally, the mind's role was as an intermediary of the spirit (or soul) and the physical body.

The role of the mind (and ego) eventually became overplayed, and so it overpowered the main pillars of human existence. And as a result, humankind became (and still is said to be) out of balance and harmony. Additionally, it also became necessary for mankind to invent the necessities of moral ethics and religion to dismantle negative thinking and behaviors that were not associated with purity. And so, many religious and social doctrines were made and brought about in an attempt to re-establish some stability and harmony in people's lives. It can also be said that the more the intellect is developed, generally speaking, the less spiritually effective mankind becomes on the whole, until people can no longer help themselves spiritually. So, it is said that there are endless calamities which are the biproducts of the overly developed mind. And these include major disasters and circumstances which prevail in humans' lives, overall.

Through the universal the laws of nature, unfortunate events may happen to people which can make them more and more intertwined in negativity. And during the early stages of development, when humanity was still pure, it is said that the High Beings frequently descended to Earth and became friends with the inhabitants there. However, when the human mind became tainted, the High Beings made only brief visits to Earth in an attempt to rescue the whole of mankind and to slowly change the future of the world. It is also said that they come to the world even now and take human form in order to teach the most pure of people the way back to their divine origins, and to try to protect all the people from the negativity which resulted in them losing their purity in the first instance.

The Integral Beings are said to be the first ancestors, the divine beginning of humanity. And even though their teachings and examples have been scattered down throughout history, their traditions have not been entirely lost. In truth, the Integral Being's teachings were left in the world as a bridge to help people to cross their own 'troubled waters.' The choice of disciplines has been very strict, too. And only those with the highest degree of sincerity, and those with the willingness to accept the responsibility for their own spiritual evolution can be received by this sacred tradition. Via purification and self-refinement is the only way one may completely unite with Tao. Every level of existence known to man can also express its own viable nature due to the specific energy formation that it contains. It is said: some beings are suitable to live in air, some in water, etc. However, all beings are produced from the same creative and generating movement energy of the universe, and this is generally referred to as Tao. All subtle differences are offspring of this primal energy, and the subtle source of the universe. Each broader classification of energy exists as a universe unto itself, with its own awareness or unawareness of time and space as a perception.

The major classifications of energy formation are the spiritual realms, the mental realm, and the physical realm, and can be referred to respectively as Heaven, Man, and Earth too, all of which make up the entire universe as a whole. The human body is said to be the microcosm of the universe connected with all three classifications of energy formation. The head incorporates Heaven, or spirit; the middle part of the chest incorporates Man, or mind; and the lower body embodies Earth, or the physical energy. Taoism also acknowledges and incorporates Divine Primacy, or what is known as the creative energy of the universe. This energy is the highest of all Heavens and is the harmonious order of the universe. It is the divine nature of creation. It is Tao.

There are multiple forms of energy within the universe. It is the original, creative energy which was twisted and distorted into many different reflections. And it is these reflections which are not the Tao. It is only the Tao that this divine tradition reveres, and it comes from the dawn of time as a divine substance which came in all the variations of the universe.

The Integral Beings were the first original, creative energy. They are the most essential and respected beings in the universe. Counting them is impossible, as the number of these beings is unfathomable. And according to the law of energy response, if there is a difficulty, the High Beings make the way to the solution. And so, the frequency of an individual's energy must be the same frequency as that of the Integral Beings. This is necessary to obtain a response from them. This connecting stream of eternal spirit responds to the divine way of self-cultivation, and an individual can refine one's energy to become the same quality as that of the Heavenly Immortals.

It can be a lifetime of understanding and pursuit to properly achieve the fullness of our truest and purest nature and connect ourselves with the Integral Realm. Therefore, we can enjoy an eternal life of happiness if we achieve Tao. The individual who is chosen to be a disciple of this divine tradition must always be very earnest and sensitive. The sacred method is vast and esoteric and cannot be passed to people with unstable natures of virtue. All offerings must be made from a sincere heart, and from service to the teacher or master (if utilizing this means as a student). All reverence must be done with utmost respectfulness to the Heavenly Shiens. The teacher or master therefore lives in this world as a bridge to mankind, and as a spiritual point of abundance of the universe.

True Taoist Practice Involves These Key Attributes

1. Simplicity
2. Patience
3. Compassion
4. Going with the Flow
5. Letting Go
6. Harmony
7. Balance

Life can become complicated quite easily, but sometimes it's really that we need to get back to the basics. When individuals feel overwhelmed, there are essential rules in how to manage actions, relationships, and self-worth.

In life, rather than fighting or pushing against the conditions in our lives, we can allow things to take their natural course of flow. This can also mean that when you don't know what to do, you may do nothing at all. Instead, only move at opportunities when you feel ready to do so.

Many Eastern philosophies remind us of the only true constants in life. These are known to be change and death. While it's not an easy thing to do, acknowledging and allowing these facts of life can release you from much suffering and also bring freedom to life. We must remember to let go, to allow life to take its course through way of flow.

The Chinese concept of yin and yang describes nature in its dualities, with two opposite, but similarly complementary and symbiotic forces. In other words, two halves can begin balancing together to make a whole. Yin and yang always flow so well, and it also changes within the expanse of time. One aspect increases as the other decreases, and this balance of power or symbiotic interdependency continues as a pattern that is seen within nature. There is a sun and a moon, a night and a day, an up and a down etc. Therefore, examining and understanding these patterns within ourselves and all around us can bring more balance in life. As an example, a person that becomes too rigid may break or explode under pressure, as a metaphor. Here, restoration of balance would occur with the addition of softness as a necessary actioning.

The 12 Fundamental Principles of Taoism

1. Tao is the Subtle Origin and Primal Energy of the Whole Universe

We recognize the Subtle Origin of the universe as the mysterious leader of both existence and non-existence. This is the yin and yang understanding or principle. To be and to not be.

The universe is natural. And according to the Tao, it was neither created nor designed by anyone. Even though there is no personified creator, the Tao is said to be the primal energy which exercises and develops itself, where the original energy becomes the subtle law of its own creation. Everything manifested and unmanifested is a miraculous expression of the nature of the Subtle Origin, where no intentional design or manipulation is necessary.

The universe is said to be an energy net of its own doing. All individual beings and things are under the influence of the energy net in the vastness of the whole. The energy net is the natural administrative system of connectedness. The freedom of all things and beings is prescribed exactly how they are meant to be.

It is said that if we indulge in our strong emotions, passions, desires, and ambitions, then the influence of the energy net will be very strong, indeed. If one's energy is light though, the influence of the energy net will also be lighter. Additionally, if an individual leads their life normally and in harmony with the universe, there will be no sign of the existence of an energy net at all.

In this world, therefore, each life is responsible only for itself. An individual may also have good fortune when his energy moves to a favorable section of the cycle for him/her. Great awareness is needed to discern whether a person is really being helped via spiritual growth, or whether he/she is just responding to the illusion of his own religious enthusiasm caused by emotional connectedness or indulgences.

2. The Tao is Absolute

Whether an individual is aware of Tao or not, all life on Earth gets their life energy from Tao. Some follow Tao consciously, knowing they are doing so. While others follow it unconsciously, without even realizing what is occurring to them. And yet, with or without awareness, Tao is the essence of all life. To be ignorant of Tao is to live without seeing. To know Tao is to see with intention. Therefore, a Taoist will follow only the absolute or the original oneness of the universe, which is the essence of life. If we violate the Tao, we destroy our own life. It is said that we cannot exist without Tao.

The eternal way is gentle. Brutal force is the low-level teaching of mind and ego perspectives. It is never the spiritual truth of a being living in a higher awareness.

3. Clarify and purify our own spirit with the outer intention to extend care and kindness to all beings and things

We refine our emotions and desires to be as light as possible, and this is so we might maintain ourselves as higher-level beings. We do not indulge in passionate love or the opposite, hate. Temper and passion are by no means our masters. In this way, we avoid any downfalls from ourselves or others.

To follow Tao is to follow the integral universe with harmonious life-giving energy. To follow emotionalism may form prejudice and nurture hostility. Because of this, people invite illness or premature death.

4. Practicing conservation with regard to our own energy

We should not waste our energy or distract our mind with frivolous, unnecessary activities. We should avoid misusing energy through arguments, restless nonsense (busy work), fidgety behavior, and pursuing the affairs of others. Doing this will preserve the integrity of our spirit and allow us to enjoy harmony with the universe. We keep a hermit's soul in a busy world.

5. We be brave and face our lives

An individual mustn't use Taoist cultivation as an escape from the reality of life, as may be the case in some religions. A simple, natural life is essential to spiritual habituality.

6. Virtue rules over materialism

The guideline of a Taoist life is to keep a clear mind's focus and have few desires which are related to resource consumption and inclusion.

7. Disallow wantonness or accumulation

Pursuit of the right purpose, right method, and right timing according to the universal subtle law of energy response. This sacred tradition can be ascertained only by disciples who lead disciplined, simple, and virtuous lives. Everything in balance, and no over consumption of any one thing or habit.

8. Sincerity, good deeds, and a purity of heart as the goal

To learn Tao, is to live a completely simple, natural, and essential life. It means we would deny unnecessary activities and be good and kind-hearted, too. From here, we allow the integration of spirit (or soul) to flow naturally.

9. The Masters of Ancient Taoist Tradition and Ch'an Buddhism are Pioneers and Examples

Looking to the great masters and teachings can help us to integrate the achievement of Tao more easily. We can learn and grow from their wisdom if we need examples within the faith or philosophy.

10. Harmony, clarity & purity of the Tao is essential

Heaviness of energy such as emotional outbursts and psychological clinginess is an obstruction to an individual's true spiritual growth. Taoism is not an ordinary religion or philosophy, by any means. In truth, most religions assume some psychological weakness for human beings from the get-go. And in this way, some followers may mistake their emotionalism for spiritualism. Additionally, many religions foster self-assertiveness, prejudice, judgment, development of ego, and hostility, too. Taoist cultivation is to integrate an individual's wholeness of being with the expansiveness of the universe.

11. Sanity is paramount in discovering and attaining Tao

Here, the development and subjective evolution of one's own beingness can occur. Without a sound mind there is no hope of attaining Tao. In fact, a state of madness is not encouraged in the path of Taoist cultivation. Criminal or scary stories, ghost stories, and even religious stories are not said to be a good source for a sound mind, unless the nature of them is to study something, but overly pursuing these is said to be non-beneficial for the mind.

12. Adopt Master Ni's works as the modernist values of ancient Taoism

Those who accept the spiritual principles given by Master Ni are recognized by the tradition as its spiritual heirs in many circles of influence. Although, the way of the Tao is not to incorporate any one set of values, but to allow for them, acknowledging their part in an individual's growth and spiritualism on the whole.

Guidelines for Service within Taoism

1. Do not tempt people with external spiritual promises.

2. Acknowledge that we are a trans-religious integral path of universal truth.

3. Following this path with the purpose of achieving universal integration is key.

4. The path is the higher guidance of the universal Divine Realm through self-awareness.

5. The path makes way and is not discriminating of names and conceptions, and directly reaches for the unnameable reality.

6. No formal doctrines, except to keep to the eternal truth of oneness.

7. No focus on worldly confusion, but instead moving to spiritual integration; the dissolving of our mind or ego self.

8. The Way does not involve discrimination and partialities which fragment human nature and unbalance (or disrupt) our involvement in life.

9. We will not create any alienation by insisting on mind or ego agendas. We see the world via an integral view.

10. We do not ascertain or push commitment from anyone who joins us. We offer ourselves to universal love as the goal. And so, we offer ourselves to all of humanity, no matter who they are or what they stand for.

11. We acknowledge our willingness to follow The Way of our own volition and understand that it is a vast process.

Chapter 3: Taoism for Beginners

So where *do* you get started? This is usually the biggest and most fundamental question asked by all newcomers to Taoism, and in a subsequent chapter, we'll be looking to explain exactly how to incorporate the wonder of Taoism into your daily modern life.

To begin properly, it is always suggested that you understand or read the Tao Te Ching by Lao Tzu, and this will be placed at the end of the title so you can make reference to the *Suggested Reading* section.

In the next section, we'll take a look at some important teachings or incorporative understandings from Lao Tzu's world-renowned title, which have been beneficially translated into English for the masses. Some Taoists have studied these sayings for years, and they are definitely profound and highly interesting. Take your time reading them, so you can fully grasp the message that is within each of them.

Excerpts as Food for Thought from the Tao Te Ching

"Simplicity, patience, compassion.

These three are your greatest treasures.

Simple in actions and thoughts, you return to the source of being.

Patient with both friends and enemies,

you accord with the way things are.

Compassionate toward yourself,

you reconcile all beings in the world."

— Lao Tzu, Tao Te Ching

"Knowing others is intelligence;

knowing yourself is true wisdom.

Mastering others is strength;

mastering yourself is true power."

— Lao Tzu, Tao Te Ching

"Those who know do not speak. Those who speak do not know."

— Lao Tzu, Tao Te Ching

When you are content to be simply yourself and don't compare or compete, everyone will respect you."

— Lao Tzu, Tao Te Ching

"The truth is not always beautiful, nor beautiful words the truth."

— Lao Tzu, Tao Te Ching

"A man with outward courage dares to die; a man with inner courage dares to live."

— Lao Tzu, Tao Te Ching

"Do you have the patience to wait until your mud settles and the water is clear?"

— Lao Tzu, Tao Te Ching

"If you understand others you are smart.

If you understand yourself you are illuminated.

If you overcome others you are powerful.

If you overcome yourself you have strength.

If you know how to be satisfied you are rich.

If you can act with vigor, you have a will.

If you don't lose your objectives you can be long-lasting.

If you die without loss, you are eternal."

— **Lao Tzu, <u>Tao Te Ching</u>**

"The flame that burns Twice as bright burns half as long."

— **Lao Tzu, <u>Tao Te Ching</u>**

"A leader is best

When people barely know he exists

Of a good leader, who talks little,

When his work is done, his aim fulfilled,

They will say, "We did this ourselves."

— **Lao Tzu, <u>Tao Te Ching</u>**

"If you try to change it, you will ruin it. Try to hold it, and you will lose it."

— **Lao Tzu, <u>Tao Te Ching</u>**

"Stop thinking, and end your problems.
What difference between yes and no?
What difference between success and failure?
Must you value what others value,
avoid what others avoid?
How ridiculous!"

— Lao Tzu, Tao Te Ching

"Other people are excited,
as though they were at a parade.
I alone don't care,
I alone am expressionless,
like an infant before it can smile."
— Lao Tzu, Tao Te Ching

"Other people have what they need;
I alone possess nothing.
I alone drift about,
like someone without a home.
I am like an idiot, my mind is so empty."
— Lao Tzu, Tao Te Ching

"Other people are bright;
I alone am dark.
Other people are sharp;
I alone am dull.
Other people have purpose;
I alone don't know.
I drift like a wave on the ocean,
I blow as aimless as the wind."
— Lao Tzu, Tao Te Ching

"I am different from ordinary people.
I drink from the Great Mother's breasts."
— Lao Tzu, Tao Te Ching

"The wise man is one who, knows, what he does not know."

— Lao Tzu, Tao Te Ching

"To understand the limitation of things, desire them."

— Lao Tzu, **Tao Te Ching**

"Give evil nothing to oppose

and it will disappear by itself."

— Lao Tzu, **Tao Te Ching**

"If you realize that all things change, there is nothing you will try to hold on to. If you are not afraid of dying, there is nothing you cannot achieve."

— Lao Tzu, **Tao Te Ching**

"All streams flow to the sea because it is lower than they are. Humility gives it its power. If you want to govern the people, you must place yourself below them. If you want to lead the people, you must learn how to follow them."

— Lao Tzu, **Tao Te Ching**

"Embracing Tao, you become embraced.

Supple, breathing gently, you become reborn.

Clearing your vision, you become clear.

Nurturing your beloved, you become impartial.

Opening your heart, you become accepted.

Accepting the World, you embrace Tao.

Bearing and nurturing,

Creating but not owning,

Giving without demanding,

Controlling without authority,

This is love."

— **Lao Tzu, <u>Tao Te Ching</u>**

"The further one goes, the less one knows."

— **Lao Tzu, <u>Tao Te Ching</u>**

"Close your mouth,
block off your senses,
blunt your sharpness,
untie your knots,
soften your glare,
settle your dust.
This is the primal identity."
— **Lao Tzu, <u>Tao Te Ching</u>**

"When people see some things as beautiful,
other things become ugly.
When people see some things as good,
other things become bad."
"He who conquers others is strong; he who conquers himself is mighty."

— **Lao Tzu, <u>Tao Te Ching</u>**

"When there is no desire,

all things are at peace."

— **Lao Tzu, <u>Tao Te Ching</u>**

"Trying to understand is like straining through muddy water. Have the patience to wait! Be still and allow the mud to settle."

— **Lao Tzu, <u>Tao Te Ching</u>**

"Hope and fear are both phantoms that arise from thinking of the self. When we don't see the self as self, what do we have to fear?"

― **Lao Tzu, <u>Tao Te Ching</u>**

"Countless words

count less

than the silent balance

between yin and yang"

― **Lao Tzu, <u>Tao Te Ching</u>**

"True words aren't eloquent;
eloquent words aren't true.
Wise men don't need to prove their point;
men who need to prove their point aren't wise.
― **Lao Tzu, <u>Tao Te Ching</u>**

The Master has no possessions.
The more he does for others,
the happier he is.
The more he gives to others,
the wealthier he is."
― **Lao Tzu, <u>Tao Te Ching</u>**

"Success is as dangerous as failure.

Hope is as hollow as fear."

― **Lao Tzu, <u>Tao Te Ching</u>**

"Love is a decision - not an emotion!"

― **Lao Tzu, <u>Tao Te Ching</u>**

"A good traveler has no fixed plans
and is not intent upon arriving.
A good artist lets his intuition
lead him wherever it wants.

A good scientist has freed himself of concepts
and keeps his mind open to what is."
— Lao Tzu, **Tao Te Ching**

"Thus the Master is available to all people
and doesn't reject anyone.
He is ready to use all situations
and doesn't waste anything.
This is called embodying the light."
— Lao Tzu, **Tao Te Ching**

"What is a good man but a bad man's teacher?
What is a bad man but a good man's job?
If you don't understand this, you will get lost,
however intelligent you are.
It is the great secret."
— Lao Tzu, **Tao Te Ching**

The Principles of Taoism Through Master Lao Tzu

Lao Tzu as the 'Master of Taoism' has influenced Chinese people for more than 2000 years. Lao Tzu wrote his profound theory of Tao, as well as the art of leading a life of wisdom. His name translates to "Old Boy" or "Old Master," and Lao Tzu is considered to be a deity by some pursuers of Tao.

We have already heard some information about Lao Tzu in the chapter above, but there is truly a need to delve in more so you can truly understand the principles of the Tao and from whom it was derived. Many Taoists state that they enjoy the connectedness to the history of the man who may (or may not) have lived on Earth, and to be a Taoist is to understand who he was, for many devout followers.

As we already know, there's a lot of speculation about the 'Master of Taoism,' namely Lao Tzu. And not much is really known about the man, in truth. He is believed to have been a teacher and a friend of Confucius and he was possibly a keeper of some archives within a smaller kingdom in China, too.

He lived around 550 B.C., but many of the details of his life have been lost throughout the passing of time. His book, *Tao Te Ching*, is the most widely translated book in the world after the *King James Bible*. His book, *Tao Te Ching*, is also known in English as the "Book of the Way." In fact, Lao Tzu's title describes the art of living harmoniously with nature and with the universe. His poetry has become classical in world literature and is the basis of the belief system for many Taoist followers around the world.

The entire philosophy of Tao was said to have begun with Lao Tzu, and it's known that some of the more religious aspects were added later on, as was discussed within this title in Chapter 1. It is believed that Lao Tzu decided to leave China, where he headed west when he was 80 years of age, because he was disappointed by his fellow countrymen and their arrogant ways of being. Before he left though, Lao Tzu was asked by a Chinese gate guard to record his beliefs and principles. The result of this request was what is now known as *Tao Te Ching*, in which Lao Tzu explains (through the use of 81 poems) the way to harmony and tranquility for those seeking The Way.

Lao Tzu may have been somewhat reclusive and contemplative, but it is said that he deeply cared about society and the state of mankind, too.

The Ideas and Philosophies of Taoism

The central belief of the Master of Taoism is that tranquility can be found by simply doing nothing. This doesn't mean that people should be passive or inactive, however. In fact, humans should stop fighting the natural flow of the universe as the main basic principle. And it has also been said, that by living in a state of constant desire, humans are guaranteed to live a life of frustration. Always wanting, needing, trying to get something or somewhere. On the other hand, however, and by letting things unfold in a natural way, individuals can find harmony with the cosmos. Stop fighting the natural flow.

It's also said that Tao cannot be described in words, and this is because Tao is said to be what existed before time and before the universe was even conceived. And so, Tao represents the infinite. And the devout followers of Tao try not to even give too much weight to the word "Tao" at all, because the word itself could, in fact, be limiting.

Lao Tzu believed that Tao is like a well, because it's empty yet filled with limitless possibility. A well is used, but it's never totally used up. Under the 'umbrella' of Taoism, humans can only be one with the universe by letting life flow naturally. This is like the ebb and flow of water, where an individual must follow the tide, rather than try to swim against the current, as a metaphor. Human beings don't even need to know their purpose in life, just as long as they simply do their work and sit back. And after that, everything else will fall into place, it is said; exactly where it should be.

Perspectives to Incorporate into Daily Life

Taoist principles are many, but there are a few basic principles that when broken down and examined, are clearly the essence to life. When you fully understand and value the importance of these principles, you are said to become Tao.

The meaning of The Way is open to debate amongst many Taoist philosophers. Some argue that it refers to your life journey or the path you choose to follow by choice, or by way of flowing with the 'tide.' All agree, however, that Taoism is an all-encompassing philosophy though, and one which offers a way for you to understand the interconnected relationship between all living things and their beginning and ending life cycles. To know the way means these things…

1. To Become the Observer

Before you can begin to understand Taoism principles, you must learn to be an observer. Observe all life around you. This task requires a level of deep contemplation and meditation, as well as physical observation that occurs without judgment. Observing nature also teaches oneness.

2. To Allow Order & Harmony

The philosophy is based in nature and the energies that keep everything in order and harmony, too. Wu-wei is the nonaction aspect of Taoism, and when the individual realizes that they are a part of the whole that makes up the overall oneness.

3. *To Learn to Observe Nature*

To understand the Taoism principles requires a deep connection with the earth and all of its elements and creatures. This can only be accomplished by learning to observe nature and begin to feel the rhythm of all life on this planet and how it is all inter-connected as a balanced whole. As the observer, your role is to note how the wind, water, air, earth, and fire are dependent upon the other for life. This same dependency is reflected throughout nature and all life in this world. The chi energy is the connecting force that cements life into one cohesive force Pu of oneness.

4. *To Become Water*

To become the first Taoism principle, you must become like the element of water. Water is passive because everything can move through it. Water doesn't resist, but by the same token, water can be a powerful mighty force that carries away life in its current. Water exemplifies the philosophy of Wu Wei, or action without action.

5. *To Know Yin & Yang*

The understanding that two opposites are completing each other in the effort to form oneness. This is clearly demonstrated in the female principle representing yin, and in the male principle representing yang. These two energies are opposite of one another, but when joined they form a completeness of energy which is known as chi. This is the governing energy of all life and the perfectly balanced form of energy in its balance.

You can accomplish "Pu" as a state of being, but only when you release preconceived ideas, including prejudices and assumptions. Here, the mind and ego are let go, and balance can be fully achieved.

6. *To Understand the Cycle of Transformation*

You can easily see the cycles of life by being the observer of it. For example, the day and night are cycling processes of the sun and the moon. The four seasons of winter, spring, summer, and fall represent the life cycles of nature in segments, which reoccur each and every year. The life cycles are made up of birth and death. The Tao is a never-ending cycle of energy transformation, and its energy never ceases to exist.

7. *To Be Harmonious*

Harmony is the natural state of beingness. Being balanced is a part of being harmonious, which means you are just as aggressive as you are passive. You are all things and nothing at the very same time. And in honesty, until you can actualize the true meaning of oneness, you cannot achieve harmony.

8. *To Be Compassionate*

The trait of compassion is necessary to understand and relate to all living life forms. When you achieve this level of empathy, you can't do any harm to any living creature. You will recognize that everything is connected and is a greater part of the whole. This is a true spiritual state of being and a genuine existence of living in harmony with all life on Earth.

9. *To Be Humble*

Living with humility means you appreciate others, even if they're different from you. You can experience a genuine respect and gratitude for those who serve as your mentors and teachers, too. And so, when you recognize that all people have value and are worthy, it is then that you will gain true humility. This recognition will incorporate all life and characterizations within the scope of life on Earth.

10. *To Achieve Balance*

Living a balanced life is the goal, and part of the teachings of Taoism. This path leads you to a life of moderation where an individual doesn't indulge in excessive living. It's also not a life of lack. Finding a true balance in life is very freeing to your soul and way of being for each day.

11. *To Live Healthily*

Living a healthy life should be an act of reverence. Refilling the well of spiritual energy is a must-do for a healthy life. Practicing different forms of meditation is essential to tapping into spiritual light and energy.

12. *To Aid Longevity*

Longevity is a part of the goals of Taoism. There are many aspects that go into creating and maintaining a longer, fuller life. This includes integrating the mind, body, and soul for balance and unison. There's a story of Peng Zu, a Tao legend, said to have last been seen when he was 800 years old. It's said that he shared his secret to longevity as being "conversation." Some believe this translated to meaning "nurturing." So, if you wish to follow in Peng Zu's footsteps, you simply *must* take care of yourself.

13. *To Be Reverent*

Reverence for ancestors is important. More specifically, the spirits of ancestors aren't the final guidepost, but a pivotal incorporation overall. This choice of remembrance and honoring is often referred to as worship. However, it's through this recognition of what ancestors gave to life that is crucial. Additionally, attending to their care in their passing will help an individual to gain more understanding of life and death.

14. *To Achieve & Understand Oneness*

When you understand Taoist incorporations, it's impossible to separate the Taoism principles from one another. They're all a part of the whole, and in unison they make up the one governing philosophy of Taoism: that of oneness.

Understanding the Yin & Yang Philosophy

Deeply rooted in ancient Chinese beliefs, this philosophy places importance on the duality of all things in the universe. In essence, this balance and harmony between yin and yang is an essential part in feng shui, some forms of martial arts, Taoism, and other eastern philosophies too.

The Beginnings of Yin and Yang in Ancient China

The imagery as a symbol of the yin and yang is recognized throughout the scope of the world. It had its beginning thousands of years ago in ancient China, in fact. The earliest symbols for yin and yang were found on oracle bones, and were dated from the 14th century B.C.

Oracle bones are the skeletal remains of animals which the early Chinese used as a method of divination. The symbology used in the inscriptions depict the innate duality of basic and natural phenomena such as day and night. Throughout the centuries thereafter, the philosophy of yin and yang also represented the beliefs of the ancient Chinese. In fact, it was a part of their understanding of the workings of the universe in its entirety. It represents the opposite, yet complementary, and dual polarity of all existence. The universe is made up of all forms of energy, or what is known as chi, and all this energy contains the balance of yin and yang.

Understanding the Philosophy of Yin and Yang

During the years 207 B.C. to 9 A.D., the Han Dynasty attempted to bring all schools of thought that existed in China. They wanted a culture which would be the standard as a philosophy, and so they tried to fuse all schools of thought into one system. The philosophers of the Han Dynasty focused on the *I Ching* which is also known as the *Book of Changes*.

The Ongoing Development of Tao

In utilizing the *I Ching*, philosophers developed the Tao, and this is the principle of the workings of the universe. In essence, the new theory was made into an appendix of the *I Ching*, and it also explains the origins of the yin and yang principles, which is also known as the *Five Agents School of Chinese Thought*. The appendix also includes an explanation of the metaphysical workings of the universe and everything within it.

The *Yin Yang School of Thought* is based on a single principle that the universe is being run by the Great Ultimate, or Tao.

The philosophy is that everything is divided into two principles that are opposite, yet dependent upon one another, too.

Meanings Found in the Yin Yang Symbol

Represented by the outer circle of the yin yang symbol is everything that's within the universe, or the whole of the singular aspect of existence. The shading of white and black shapes that are within the circle represent the duality. And it's these shapes which symbolize the two energies, and their interaction with each other that causes everything in the universe to occur. The flowing curvy shapes are representative of the constant change that takes place in the universe between yin and yang, with one flowing into the other in an infinite cycle of balance and harmony.

Yin and Yang Are Present in Everything That Exists

According to the yin yang philosophy, each is present in everything that exists. The yin yang sign represents this effortlessly. The large dark area has a small and white circle, and the white area has a small and dark circle. This shows through symbology that; just as it is in life, everything is not completely white or black, and neither one can exist alone either. They must, in fact, exist together, and each energy contains elements of its opposite energy.

Interaction Among the Opposite Energies

The symbol gives the feeling of the strong interaction of the two opposing energies, effortlessly showing how there's a continual movement and exchange of energy between them, just as there is a constant exchange of the energies within all life.

The Spectrum of Energy which Exists

From the yin and yang principle, there exists a spectrum of energies that flow from one to the other, eternally.

For example, let's use the running of bathwater to just the right temperature before you get in. When you turn the tap purely to hot, it's too heated, so you might also add a bit of cold to the hot water to adjust the temperature. The bathwater therefore exists on the spectrum of temperature, and so it contains elements of the polar opposites within the temperature spectrum, namely hot and cold.

Let's do another example to explain it further. The human brain is divided into two halves, the left and the right, with each half controlling different functions of your mind. Your left-brain controls the areas which are associated with thought and reason, while the right-brain controls the areas associated with intuition and creativity. So, to have a fully functioning mind, you need both of these aspects, otherwise you can't complete creative tasks without reasoning, and you can't adequately think through a solution without an element of intuition. The blending of these two opposite energies creates the whole of your mind. They are opposite, yet complementary.

Components of Yin and Yang

Yin:
- Moon
- Passive
- Reception
- Weak
- Completion
- Submission
- Contradicting
- Small
- Night
- Up & down movement
- Death
- Withdrawn
- Cold
- Moist

Yang:
- Sun
- Heaven
- Bright
- Dominance
- Light
- Hot
- Active
- Forceful
- Heat
- Dry
- Birth

- Large
- Strong
- Expanding
- Day
- An up and out movement

Presence in Absence

Based on the philosophy of yin and yang, everything within the known universe is cyclical and constant. This means that one opposing force dominates for a part of time, and then the opposing force becomes the dominant one for a part of time. It also means that in each state are 'seeds' of the opposing force. As an example, in light are the 'seeds' of darkness. Everything (therefore) contains principles of its equal opposite, and in philosophical terms this is known as *presence in absence*.

The following are more examples of yin and yang which are seen throughout the universe:

- Sickness and health
- Life and death
- Power and submission
- Dominance and submission
- The cycle of the seasons as hot replaces cold
- A violent storm followed by stillness and calm
- Day and night
- Light and dark

- Land and ocean
- Wealth and poverty
- Expansion and implosion

The Yin and Yang Philosophy Represents Duality

The yin and yang philosophy can really describe the duality found in everything in the universe, and this includes the interactions of opposing energies as being existential. It's present everywhere, and each component is neither good nor bad, it just is. One part cannot exist without the other, however. And it's also true too, that no judgment is given as to whether or not it's good or evil, right or wrong, good or bad, etc. It just simply is.

Chapter 4: Advanced Actions to Accentuate Your Practices

The I Ching

The *I Ching* has served for thousands of years as a taxonomy of the universe, a philosophical guide to an ethical life, a manual for rulers, and an oracle of an individual's personal future and the future of the state.

Historically, it was an organizing principle or what's known as an authoritative proof for literary and arts criticism, medicine, cartography, and many of the sciences as well. It also generated Confucian, Taoist, Buddhist, and later, even Christian additions, and other competing schools of thought within the traditions mentioned.

In China and within East Asia, it's one of the most consulted of all books, in the belief that it can explain absolutely everything. In the West though, it's been around for over 300 years. Since the 1950s, it's been the most popularly recognized Chinese book around, along with the *Tao Te Ching*.

With its infinite applications and interpretations, there's never been a book quite like it anywhere in the world. It's an epicenter of a vast whirlwind of writings and practices, and is also a continually shifting work, because most of the crucial words of the *I Ching* have no fixed meaning.

The origin of the text is quite obscure. In the mythological version, the culture hero is known as Fu Xi, and is a dragon or a snake with a human face. He studied the patterns of nature in the sky and on the earth too, including the markings on rocks, birds, and animals, as well as the movement of clouds, and the arrangement of the stars. He discovered that everything could be reduced to just eight trigrams, where each is composed of 3 stacked, solid, or broken lines, reflecting the yin and yang meanings, the opposite and complementing dualities that drive the universe. The trigrams represent heaven, a lake, fire, thunder, wind, water, a mountain, and earth.

Fu Xi included all aspects of civilization including kingship, marriage, writing, agriculture, and navigation, and it's said that he taught these to his human descendants.

The *I Ching* mythology turns into legend, too. And in (approximately) the year 1050 BCE, and according to the tradition of that time, Emperor Wen, founder of the Zhou dynasty, doubled the trigrams to hexagrams (six-lined figures). He then numbered and arranged all the possible combinations. In total there are 64, and he gave them all names.

Emperor Wen also wrote brief oracles for each that are now known as the "Judgments." His son, namely the Duke of Zhou, was a poet, and he added gnomic interpretations for the individual lines of each hexagram. It was said that, around 500 years later, Confucius wrote ethical commentaries explicitly for each hexagram, which are called the "Ten Wings."

Around circa 1600 BCE, or possibly even earlier, fortune-telling diviners would add heat to tortoise shells or the scapulae of oxen to interpret the cracks that were produced from doing this ancient practice. Many of these oracle bones were unearthed in archaeology. Some have complete hexagrams, or the numbers assigned to hexagrams placed upon them. The history of the oracle bones is completely unknown.

It was within the Zhou dynasty, circa 800 BCE, that the 64 hexagrams were named, and a written text was established based upon the spoken traditions. The book became known as the *Zhou Yi*.

The process of consultation also began from the use of tortoise shells, and this required an expert to perform the methodology and to interpret it. Now there's the system of coins or yarrow stalks that anyone can practice, and it's been in use ever since. In modern times, 3 coins with numbers assigned to heads or tails are simultaneously tossed. The sum indicates a solid or broken line, and 6 proper coin tosses produces a hexagram. For yarrow stalks, 50 are counted out to produce the number for each line.

Around the 3rd century BCE, the rise of Confucianism and the "Ten Wings" commentaries had been added in, allowing the *Zhou Yi* to become something far more magical, changing from a strictly divinatory manual to a highly revered philosophical and morality-driven text.

In around 135 BCE, Emperor Wu of the Han dynasty declared it to be the most important of the 5 canonical Confucian books and he standardized the text. This title became known as the *I Ching, the Book of Change*, and its format has remained the same ever since that time period. It's important to understand that Confucius had nothing to do with the making of the *I Ching*, but he did supposedly say that, "If I had another hundred years to live, fifty of them would be devoted to studying it."

The study of the *I Ching* is an important refence with regards to Taoism. As an advanced pupil, it would be incomprehensible to not look at it to add to the current practices, teachings, and understandings, even if utilized only for study purposes.

In truth, it was said to be the essential guide to the universe. And in a philosophical universe where everything is connected, and everything is in a state of restless change. And so, the book was not a mere description of the cosmos, but an understanding of the perfect microcosm. And with its 64 hexagrams; became the categories for countless disciplines. Its mysterious "Judgments" were taken as 'seeds' of thought to be elaborated, and this is true with regard to the "Ten Wings" and countless commentaries added. There is also advice to rulers on how to run an orderly state, and for ordinary people on how to live a proper, better life. Also used as a tool for meditation on the universe and as a seamless piece of the way of the world, the book also spoke of what might be auspicious or inauspicious for the future.

In the West, however, the *I Ching* was discovered in the late 17th century by some Jesuit missionaries in China, and these missionaries decoded the book to reveal its Christian universal truth.

They believed that hexagram number 1 was God; 2 was the second, namely Adam, and Jesus the third (or the 3) being the Trinity. Then 8, the members of Noah's family, and on and on they decoded it to match up with Christianity.

Leibniz was one who enthusiastically found the universality of his own binary system in the solid and broken lines. Whereas Hegel considered the book as being "superficial." And he stated "There is not to be found in one single instance a sensuous conception of universal natural or spiritual powers."

The first English translation was by Canon Thomas McClatchie, an Anglican in Hong Kong. McClatchie was a revered figure, and in 1876, found the key to all mythologies and ascertained that the *I Ching* had been brought to China by one of Noah's sons and that it was a "pornographic" celebration of a "hermaphroditic monad."

James Legge, also a missionary in Hong Kong and a man who loathed China, was the first important English-language translator of the Chinese classics and considered McClatchie to be "delirious." Unfortunately, though, after 20 interrupted years of work on the translation, the manuscript was lost in a shipwreck in the Red Sea. Legge did produce the first reliable English translation of the *I Ching* in 1882, and was the one that first applied the English word for a six-pointed star to the lines, now also to be known as "hexagram."

Legge found himself "...gradually brought under a powerful fascination," and it led him to devise a well-rounded theory of translation. And since Chinese characters were not "representations of words, but symbols of ideas, the combination of them in composition is not a representation of what the writer would say, but of what he thinks." The translator must become "*en rapport*" with the author and enter into a "seeing of mind to mind," or a "participation" in the thoughts of the author that goes beyond what the author seemingly said. Although the *I Ching* has no, one author, Legge's version is covered with explanations and clarifications which are inserted into an otherwise literal translation of the text.

Herbert Giles was the next important English-language translator after Legge, and he thought the *I Ching* was "apparent gibberish." He went onto say that "This is freely admitted by all learned Chinese, who nevertheless hold tenaciously to the belief that important lessons could be derived from its pages if only we had the wit to understand them."

Arthur Waley, in a 1933 study; he described it as a collection of "peasant interpretation" or omens to which specific divinations had been added at a later date. He never fully interpreted the book, however. He also wrote that the omen "red sky in the morning, shepherds take warning" would become the divination and changed it to "red sky in the morning: inauspicious; do not cross the river."

Arthur Waley found 3 categories of omens: "...inexplicable sensations and involuntary movements ('feelings,' twitchings, stumbling, belching and the like)...those concerning plants, animals and birds...[and] those concerning natural phenomena (thunder, stars, rain etc.)" He also found examples of all of them during his study of the book.

Next was Joseph Needham who was thoroughly devoted and said many exasperated pages to the *I Ching* in *Science and Civilization in China* were merely a "pseudo-science" that had, for centuries, a minimalistic effect on *actual* Chinese science, which attempted to fit exacting observations into the "cosmic filing-system." He also mentioned the vagueness of categories of the hexagrams.

It was Richard Wilhelm's 1924 German translation of the *I Ching* which transformed the text from humble to international stardom. Wilhelm was a missionary in China and a true believer in the wisdom of the East, saying China was the wisest of all. The "relentless mechanization and rationalization of life in the West" needed the "Eastern adhesion to a natural profundity of soul." And so, it was his overall mission to get people to "join hands in mutual completion," to uncover the "common foundations of humankind" so that it would be possible to "find a core in the innermost depth of the humane, from where we can tackle...the shaping of life."

Referencing the *I Ching* is an important part of Taoism. Not only does it incorporate the Chinese traditions, but it has writings from multiple masters and teachers who were philosophers and important creators of that time.

Just as the *Tao Te Ching* is important for appraisal and study, the study of the history of Taoism is too, including its philosophies, belief systems, and nuances, including major texts of comparison and agreement. This is part of the nature of Taoism.

It was Richard Wilhelm's translation that relied upon the Song Dynasty Neo-Confucian interpretations of the words as a proper translation. In the name of universality, where, more specifically, Chinese referents were given general terms, and the German edition had scores of footnotes too. These were said to be "parallels" to Goethe, the German Romantics, Kant, and even the Bible. These incorporations were dropped for the English language, however.

The book carried an *Introduction* by Carl Jung too, who Wilhelm stated to be "in touch with the findings of the East [and] in accordance with the views of the oldest Chinese wisdom." One of the parts included Jung's male and female principles, the *anima* and the *animus*, which Wilhelm connected to the *yin* and *yang*. Some of Jung's assertions were revered. "It is a curious fact that such a gifted and intelligent people as the Chinese have never developed what we call science." But also notable was his emphasis on chance and synchronicity, the *Jungian*, or metaphysical version of chance which was, at the time, something new, even if, and for true believers, the *I Ching* did not operate on chance at all.

It was the Wilhelm/Baynes/Bollingen edition which made a stir in the 1950s and 60s. Here, Allen Ginsberg, Octavio Paz, Jorge Luis Borges, and Charles Olson, among others, wrote poetry which was inspired by its poetic language. Fritjof Capra in *The Tao of Physics* used it to explain quantum mechanics and Terence McKenna found that its geometrical patterning looked similar to the 'chemical waves' produced by hallucinogens. Others too, heavily considered the *I Ching's* binary system of lines to be a prototype for what is now known as the personal computer (or PC).

The innovative and thrilling the arrival of the *I Ching* was a product of art and culture to the West. It brought much of the mysterious East, and what Wilhelm called "the seasoned wisdom of thousands of years." It was an ancient book without any real or true author, a wonderment, a purposeful configuration with no beginning and no end, and also a religious text with no deities, gods, or priests to have to submit to. Instead, it was a do-it-yourself divination that required no experienced diviner. It was a self-help book for those who wouldn't be caught reading self-help books, and one that provided an exciting glimpse of one's personal future. It was also, according to world-famous Bob Dylan, "...the only thing that is amazingly true."

John Minford, a scholar best known for his 5-volume translation of *The Story of the Stone (also known as The Dream of the Red Chamber)* and is universally considered to be the best Chinese novel in the world. Additionally, a project which was begun by the late David Hawkes.

Each portion of the entries for each hexagram is accompanied by a digest of the historical commentaries and the interpretations given by previous translators, as well as reflections by Minford too, which link the hexagram to

Chinese poetry, ritual, art, history, mythology, and philosophy. A read that's well worth the wait.

David Hinton is a rare example of a literary sinologist. A sinologist is a classical scholar thoroughly conversant and connected to contemporary literature within the English language. Both he and Watson are said to be the most important American translators of Chinese classical poetry and philosophy within the last century, in fact. Both are immensely profound as they journey into language and text, and both have introduced completely new ways of translating Chinese poetry. In fact, Hinton's *I Ching* is equally as inventive as it is quite short, with only two pages allotted to each hexagram given, presenting a few excerpts from the original "Ten Wings". And rather than a consultation or ideology of what is written, it is meant to be read cover to cover, like a book of modern poetry, although it should be meant as a translation, and not an idea or an elaboration of what is already there.

Interestingly too, Hinton complies with the Taoist or Ch'an (Zen) Buddhist interpretation of the book and is unconcerned with the Confucian ethical and political pushes. His version of *I Ching* puts the reader into the Tao that relates to nature, up to and including the way of the world as it's portrayed by nature and embodied by the title, in essence. He additionally takes the mysterious lines of the "Judgments" as precursors to the later Taoist and Ch'an writings, stating that they are "strategies…to tease the mind outside workaday assumptions and linguistic structures, outside the limitations of identity." His idea of *I Ching* is the opposite of Wilhelm's Jungian self-realization methodology, and instead, it's intended as a profound realization of selflessness. Also, it's intrinsically based on the belief that ancient Chinese culture, including living closer to the land, is less estranged from nature's Tao.

Interestingly too, Hinton sometimes translates according to a pictographic reading of the oldest characters, and this is an avid technique which was first used by Ezra Pound in his earliest Chinese poetry anthology known as the *Book of Songs*, which he titled *The Confucian Odes*. To compare, Hinton calls Hexagram 32 "Moondrift Constancy," but it's usually translated to "Endurance," "Duration," or "Perseverance." Some sinologists would call Hinton's translation treachery, and therefore negate his interpretation altogether.

Minford translates hexagram 52 as "Mountain" because the hexagram is composed of the two mountain-like trigrams, one atop the other. His translation of the text throughout the book is said to be minimalist too, with each line centered, rather than pushed left. Minford incorporates tags in Latin, which were taken from the early Jesuit translations, and which he states can help individuals to be able to relate to this foreign text, and also create a timeless mood for contemplation to occur.

In the "Book of Wisdom" segment, he translates the "Judgment" for Hexagram 52 to mean: *"The back is still as a mountain; There is no body. He walks in the courtyard, unseen. No Harm,* Nullum malum."

This is followed by an interesting inception about the spiritual role and poetic image of mountains within the Chinese tradition.

David Hinton calls the hexagram "Stillness" and translates it: "Stillness in your back. Expect nothing from your life. Wander the courtyard where you see no one. How could you ever go astray?"

Wilhelm states it as: "Keeping still, mountain" as the name of the hexagram. And his version of "Judgment" states: *"Keeping still. Keeping his back still so that he no longer feels his body. He goes into the courtyard and does not see his people. No blame."*

He explains it as the "true quiet," in fact, which means keeping still when the time has come to keep still and moving forward when the time has come to move forward. And so, the rest and movement are in agreement with the demands placed there by time, and that there is light in life. He adds too, that the hexagram signifies the end and beginning of all movement. Additionally, the back is named so because in the back are located all the nerve fibers that allow for true physical movement. And if the movement of these spinal nerves is brought to a stop, then the ego, with its restlessness, can (and will) disappear. When an individual becomes calm, it is only then that the individual may turn to the outside world. The person no longer sees in it the struggle and tumultuousness of individual beings, and so has that true peace of mind which is needed for understanding. Here, the great laws of the cosmos can be in harmony with the individual. Whomever acts from these deeper levels makes no mistakes within their life.

Questions Related to Text for Included & Important Thought

The texts related to Taoism are few really. But historically, there are two that bring Taoist followers much joy and intrigue. It is also true that the translations from the Chinese language are many, and notable. To read one translation of the text in another language could have a huge impact on what the true author (or authors) had intended. And so, reading many translations of the texts can be beneficial, so that more than one perception might be understood and thoroughly thought about at length.

After reading, it's also truly important that individuals can reflect upon what's been read and understood, or not understood at the time of perception. Remembering too, that perceptions can change over time.

It's also true that many Taoists spend years trying to understand the teachings of such sacred texts. In fact, this alone can take up a lifetime for many who are devoted to The Tao, The Way.

And so, as an advanced practice of Taoism, the study of texts relating to it are essential, and could be expressed as the life and breath of knowing more, being more, gaining more, and filling the spiritual self with more. And so, an invitation to posing some questions might also ensue now, and a comparison of religious practices and texts might also be quite fulfilling for you, the reader. An individual might like to read the Holy Quran, the Bible, and other religious texts too, and compare them to validate more of an understanding and comparison to Taoism as a philosophy and as a religion. In fact, the least common denominator with regards to Taoism is the salvation ideal, which is not present for Taoism as it is within other religions. And this might be the reason it's become so popular in modern times, for the simple reason that there is no quest after life is passed, and that for right now, life is all there is. In fact, the exploration of death is simply not important, because we are living.

So, what do other texts say about all of these things, life and death, good and evil, night and day, etc? Let's take a moment to delve a little bit deeper, so that we might incorporate more as we learn and compare Taoism as both a religion and a philosophy. Some added texts will also be added to the *Suggested Reading* list at the end of this title. Some volumes will be available as eBooks and some might only be available as physical copies. Check your local stores to find out. Reading is gratifying too, mentally and spiritually speaking.

It's important for a person to ponder these questions for themselves as an individual:

For the Tao Te Ching

What is the *Tao Te Ching* for you?

What characterizes *Tao Te Ching* for you?

How might you describe the nature of opposites and relationships as portrayed in the *Tao Te Ching*?

How would you begin to compare the themes of the *Tao Te Ching* to the Bhagavad Gita? To the Dhammapada? To Hinduism? To Buddhism? To Confucianism?

What most surprised you about the *Tao Te Ching*?

Are there particular passages that stand out for you in the *Tao Te Ching*? Why?

What metaphors are used in the *Tao Te Ching*? How do these fit with the overall approach and meanings overall?

To what extent does the *Tao Te Ching* have a sense of divinity? Is there a concept of God embedded within the *Tao Te Ching* or not?

What does this title have to say about society? About ruling? About the people?

For the I Ching

What is the *I Ching* to you?

What characterizes the *I Ching* for you?

How might you describe the *I Ching*?

How would you begin to compare the themes of the *I Ching* to the Bhagavad Gita? To the Dhammapada? To Hinduism? To Buddhism? To Confucianism?

What most surprised you about the *I Ching*?

Are there particular passages that stand out for you in the *I Ching*? Why?

What metaphors are used in the *I Ching*? How do these fit in with the overall approach and meanings overall?

To what extent does the *I Ching* have a sense of divinity? Is there a concept of God embedded within the *I Ching* or not?

What does this title have to say about society? About ruling? About the people?

For the Bible

What is the *Bible* to you?

What characterizes the *Bible* for you?

How might you describe the *Bible?*

How would you begin to compare the themes of the *Bible* to the Bhagavad Gita? To the Dhammapada? To Hinduism? To Buddhism? To Confucianism?

What most surprised you about the *Bible*?

Are there particular passages that stand out for you in the *Bible*? Why?

What metaphors are used in the *Bible*? How do these fit in with the overall approach and meanings overall?

To what extent does the *Bible* have a sense of divinity? Is there a concept of God embedded within the *Bible* or not?

What does this title have to say about society? About ruling? About the people?

For the Holy Quran

What is the *Holy Quran* to you?

What characterizes the *Holy Quran* for you?

How might you describe the *Holy Quran*?

How would you begin to compare the themes of the *Holy Quran* to the Bhagavad Gita? To the Dhammapada? To Hinduism? To Buddhism? To Confucianism?

What most surprised you about the *Holy Quran*?

Are there particular passages that stand out for you in the *Holy Quran*? Why?

What metaphors are used in the *Holy Quran*? How do these fit in with the overall approach and meanings overall?

To what extent does the *Holy Quran* have a sense of divinity? Is there a concept of God embedded within the *Holy Quran* or not?

What does this title have to say about society? About ruling? About the people?

Add in These Helpful Practices to Enhance Taoism Overall:

Meditation

Meditation is important to many avid Taoists. Complex meditation rituals are practiced in various temples, too. The vital use of meditation is to create mental stillness and to enhance mindfulness as a daily practice. This can give a person the mental space to know the Tao, both indirectly and directly.

As you practice your time of mediation, your first 4 energy bodies (physical, etheric, mental, and emotional) will start to balance out. In fact, by developing and working with these first 4 energy bodies, it truly enhances a solid foundation to go deeper and take meditation to more advanced levels. This is so you can become a free, conscious, spiritual being.

In monasteries and deep in parts of Western China, Taoists developed a complete and exact science of meditation. They developed advanced methods for those who were ready, in fact. This includes what is known as the *Inner Dissolving Method*, sexual meditation, and inner alchemy.

The 1 Million Agendas

Many individuals have issues or agendas that they want to directly address. People have many agendas, and this has always been true. Maybe it's that a person had a terrible childhood, has recently been through a break-up, or they might be missing a loved one.

The 1 Million Agendas is a useful way to approach meditation for a specific purpose. Here we can say that: an agenda is anything you want to address because you know enough is enough, and that you want to be rid of it, finally; once and for all. The content of an agenda can be whatever you desire it to be. One application of the *Inner Dissolving Method* is to let go of whatever needs to fall away.

You can make the purpose of the agenda whatever comes up in your life that's worrying you, no matter what it might be or how it's manifesting into an agenda, per say. And as you do the method, you can dissolve it from your life with purposeful intention. This technique involves the way you move your energy within, and it does so via emotional attachment. It starts by activating your intent and progressing further and deeper.

Formulating an Agenda: Preparing for Meditation

If you want your mind to be magnetized toward one agenda, you must contemplate it before you begin the dissolving process. If you do so during the day (or an hour before you practice), it's usually enough time. Or, as an alternative, you could focus for the next few minutes on the emotion that's associated with your agenda as you scan downward. You could also think about a specific situation that you're holding onto that you don't want anymore. Maybe you might think about how someone deceived you, or perhaps how you lost in a situation when you expected to win.

Pick an agenda and focus upon it. Now you can go about starting to release your agenda in one of two ways:

1. You can keep on thinking about that emotion in general.

2. You can think about a particular issue that you have in relationship to that emotion.

Either way, you're formulating an agenda towards the issue. It doesn't matter, really; as long as your mind is focusing on a particular emotion, your energy will start moving toward where it is inside of you. In that part or section of the physical body you will feel it. When you truly become free inside, you will no longer experience this pull, hurt, or stagnancy.

Experiencing the full range of emotions is completely natural and healthy, but as your ability to dissolve agendas increases, you won't experience the spikes where you might have once erupted in anger, burst into tears, or jumped with elation with little or no stimulus. You will just flow from one emotion to the next, eventually, and your emotional response will be more proportional to the positive or negative experiences themselves. Practice makes perfect here, and doing so safely, in the comfort of your own home, let's say, well, this allows you to feel safe, too.

Diet Consideration

Historically, the Taoist diet has consisted of mainly fresh fruits and vegetables, with very little meat and no grain at all. We'll look more into the dietary considerations in a future chapter, however. The reason for the no grain ruling though, was that the Chinese thought that during the digestive process that demon-like creatures could be released from the rotting grain, and perhaps attempt to eat them from the inside out.

Belief System Changes

Incorporation of Chinese religion associated with the *Tao Te Ching* and *I Ching* texts, where both philosophical and political texts incorporate guidelines and teachings for the follower. Taoist ideas have become popular throughout the world through Tai Chi Chuan, Qigong, and various martial arts, too. Taoism is an ancient tradition of philosophy and is also said to be a religious belief that is deeply rooted in Chinese customs and a wider worldview overall.

Incorporation of beliefs will need to incorporate what follows, below:

1. Humanity

The primary focus based on the individual's spiritual existence, where his/her humanity is believed to be like a bamboo stick. It's straight and simple by design, but it has a vacant center that yearns to be filled and is flexible enough to overcome resistance, and to also resist the blows of nature by way of being.

2. Yin Yang

A basic belief using the universal energy of chi, the life-giving force drawn from the powerful interchange of the polar forces known as yin and yang. The flow of chi is an essential element of life's flow or continuity; it is believed to support and give prosperity, and health, good fortune, by way of simultaneously blocking sickness, conflicts, and difficulties, too. Here, the constant flow of chi guarantees the welfare of individuals and the world in which they live, and it does so by using the combination of Taoist doctrine with a participant expression of Chinese spirituality. Additionally, every action creates a counteraction by itself, therefore, its natural and unavoidable movement.

3. Man's Will

The man's (or woman's) will is not solely responsible. That is to say that: it isn't considered as the root problem in Taoism. Rather, it's more widely believed that the individual must place their will in harmony with the natural universe.

Additionally, Taoist philosophy believes that the cosmos already works in harmony in its own ways, and if a person exerts his will against the world, then he/she would cause disruption to the harmony that already exists, and so the individual should go with the flow of life.

4. The 3 Jewels of Tao

(i) Compassion, kindness, and love

(ii) Moderation, simplicity, and frugality

(iii) Humility and modesty

5. The 5 Basic Movements

Within Taoism, matter and energy are considered completely governed by the 5 basic movements with regards to the elements. The strength and influence of these movements waxes and wanes over the course of a year, however, with wood peaking during the spring, fire during the summer, metal in the fall, water in the winter, and then the earth aspect too. The earth asserts its presence most powerfully during the periods of the start of each season.

6. Belief in Deity

Taoists also believe that the supreme being (known as ultimate truth) is beyond words or any possible understanding, and so they name it The Tao or The Way. The power of The Way is referred as the "Te." These Tao and Te are the central concepts of Taoism. Tao is described as the divine way of the entire universe, and Te is the power of Tao and the power to bring Tao into realization. It also incorporates the belief that human interference can be damaging and limiting.

7. Incarnation and Death

Taoists do not believe that the God resembled a human, nor do they have any particular meaning or thought about death. Taoism teaches that humans should accept life and death as being complementary to each other, and so, they are important aspects of The Tao or The Way. Death should not be feared but should also not be desired. Life and death in Taoism are like yin and yang, or what might be said as going from being to non-being.

8. Good and Evil

Good and evil is the interdependence of all the dualities. To understand the notion of good and evil like a Taoists does, an individual would need to be able to differentiate between the 'concept' of evil and the 'reality' of evil. Taoists say that: when someone labels something as being "good," then they automatically create an evil. Any action is merely expected to have some negativity (yin) and some positivity (yang).

9. Salvation

As a practice, Taoist followers do not believe in salvation, and they don't have any practices regarding this, in fact. They believe that there's nothing that an individual should be saved from, and the belief in salvation means that one believes in damnation too; in the same manner as the belief in good also results in the belief of evil. Taoists believe that not excessively pursuing material wealth or prestige will lead to a more joyful life, however.

10. Immortals

The primary importance is given to the Immortals or Xian as known in Chinese tradition. In the Chuang-Tzu, these perfect beings are known to dwell far away in a peaceful place, where they experience an effortless, easy existence. They're believed to be ageless too, and the spiritual beings are believed to eat nothing but air, and to drink nothing but dew, and they also enjoy the power of flight. These beings are powerful and believed to be revered within the group of Eight Immortals, who are said to have been born during the period of the Tang Dynasty.

Acting with Purity & Intention

Do not be over-indulgent or think depraved thoughts. Do not steal or receive unrighteous wealth by way of lying or greed invocation. Do not cheat or misrepresent good and evil. Do not get intoxicated, and always think of pure conduct in each day of life.

Add in Reverence or Worship

The highest god/principle is the Tao. There's no compulsion to worship them, although some Taoists do. There's no compulsion to pray to them, although some Taoists do. Typical prayer at a Taoist shrine might be addressed to Taoist gods and involve incense, money, and bowing; and may or may not involve any spoken dialogue.

Chapter 5: The Way of Internals for a Healthful Body

The process of being and doing is a necessity for incorporation. Understanding the link between spirituality and movement is the key here. In this chapter, we will discover more and more about what is necessary for Taoist practice and conformity. The physical body can be greatly improved as we understand this link, too.

Internal and External Alchemy

Taoist practices which are physical, such as breath exercises, martial arts, massage, yoga, and meditation are all designed to transform a person in multiple ways. In fact, each practice does so both mentally and physically, and so brings the individual into closer harmony with Tao (The Way).

"The whole thrust of Taoism has always been in terms of healing methods that seek to re-establish the original balanced wholeness of human nature and society." - **Norman Girardot**

Many of these practices are called internal alchemy (known as *nei-dun*), and Taoists also practice external alchemy (known as *wai-dan*), which involves improvements in diet and the use of minerals and herbs to promote longer life as well as a quality of life.

So Why is it Called Alchemy?

Alchemists are people who want to transform things into something more valuable, such as converting lead into gold. Taoist alchemy is concerned with transforming human beings so as to give them longer life and bring them closer to Tao.

The first alchemists were all about seeking an elixir which could be used to turn cheap metal into gold. They worked in laboratories, and worked on grinding, mixing, and heating various substances together in search of the magical compound. Other alchemists went in search of a different sort of elixir; a pill, potion or a practice that might make human beings' immortal.

Creating an elixir also involved various combinations of ingredients and particular methods of heating, grinding, and mixing, together with other rituals and ways of alchemy practice. This became known as *wai-dan* (or external alchemy) presumably because it involved adding something to the body from the outside. It was both a literal idea, since some people must have hoped to live for ever, and a metaphorical one, in which the spirit was steadily purified and came closer to unity with Tao.

Interior alchemy, which didn't involve external physical compounds, was probably developed slightly later. For a long time, both were practiced together (rather in the same way that some modern patients will use both drugs and meditation to deal with sickness). This inner and outer alchemy was popular, and still is, even in today's modern practice of Taoism.

Interior (or inner) alchemy also seeks to achieve longer life, purity, and a closeness to Tao, but the practitioner works on themselves without the use of chemicals to transform the elements within their body into purer forms that will promote the energy of life.

The older texts retain the alchemical link by using the language of making an elixir, and of chemical transformation to describe internal spiritual development.

Agendas & Your Internal Organs

When you start thinking about a certain emotion, an individual can rub or press against the corresponding organ to help make them aware of the ways in which emotions can also be a bodily experience. In fact, certain organs are linked to certain emotions.

- Fear is linked to the kidneys
- Grief is linked to the lungs
- Anxiety is linked to the heart
- Anger is linked to the liver

Take time to think about a certain agenda for 5 to 10 minutes before you start your meditation. Additionally, you can think about why you hold on to this issue. After 10 minutes, you may let your mind completely relax. Let everything be calm and go out of your mind for a time. Sit and wait. At some point, you may get a lighter sense of the emotions associated with your particular agenda, or at least some sense of it beginning inside of your body somewhere.

Start now and make the intention to move from the top of your head and dissolve the feelings and then continue down to the bottom of your belly. As you dissolve down from the top of your head, keep feeling for the energy behind whatever comes into your awareness. Thoughts will come to mind and you will start talking to yourself from your inner mind. It's very important that you don't try to edit the thoughts that come. In fact, it's important to stay with the energy that's behind them.

After a time, you can find yourself going into an entirely different place, an inner world, another 'place' than where you've ever been before. Let whatever thoughts or conversations you are having in your head come up for you but stay aware of the energy behind these inner conversations.

Keep dissolving and staying focused on the energy behind what you are feeling now.
Some agendas might be:

1. Anxiety
2. Grief
3. Greed
4. Fear
5. Depression
6. Loss
7. Forgiveness
8. Anger
9. Pain, either physical, emotional, or mental

The Taoist Water Method of the Inner Dissolving Process is Key

The *Taoist Water Method* involves dissolving and resolving the bound blockages of your first 6 energy bodies until you become internally free. And this is an exciting and exceptional experience.

Here, we can say that the outer and inner dissolving processes begin when you consciously use your awareness to focus your mind. You do this on any specific condensed energy shape or patterning within yourself. After this, you can then dissipate that shape until it no longer obstructs the mind, body, or the spirit (soul).

The outer dissolving process is: "ice to water, water to gas." "Ice" is a reference to the blocked and congealed energy. "Water" is a reference to the acceptance and relaxing of the internal blockage until it no longer causes you tension. And "gas" refers to the complete release of all the bound energy that was originally there, which is moving away from your physical body. If it's not completely released, the energy may revert to "ice." Be aware of this for future meditations. Sometimes you may think an agenda is resolved, but it might need more time.

The Inner Dissolving Process

For comparison, the inner dissolving process of the *Water Method* is "ice to water, water to space." And here, "space" means the vast internal space that exists within the physical body. This is the space which is as infinite as the cosmos.

In the "ice to water" phase of the outer dissolving process, the solid, completely bound and condensed shape is a metaphor, where "ice" is released until it relaxes and reaches the surface of the skin as "water."

The inner dissolving process is where the stuck or bound energy is also released at the pinpoint of the blockage, and until it becomes relaxed, soft, and like "water." Water can revert back to ice at any stage. So, this method might need to be used regularly to stop this from occurring as mentioned previously.

Releasing Stuck or Blocked Energy

Your "liquid" energy might move in two different directions:

1. In the outer dissolving process, you release your blocked chi from your skin to the outside of your physical body, and then to the edge of your chi/etheric body. Sometimes you move it beyond this as a reflection of the "water to gas" practice or process. The previously condensed energy is now balanced, unblocked, and shapeless too.

2. When you move to the "water-space" section of the inner dissolving process, you release the blocked (and felt) sensations by imploding your energy. This energy moves into the inner space that your original, condensed, and blocked energy shape once occupied. This state is consciousness or emptiness.

During the beginning part of the sitting meditation, it's important that the individual dissolves a blockage well. Here, the release of energy goes inward, and deeper into the internal space (the consciousness). The Taoist thought on this is that: there is as much internal space inside of you as there is space in the whole external universe. The cosmos is inside of you. This is a mind-blowing thought, especially if you've never really thought about it before.

Eventually, as a Taoist practice, the inner and outer dissolving processes are combined, so that as the individual dissolves inward, either sequentially or simultaneously, the individual also dissolves outwardly and toward the outer physical world, out into the universe. After a time, this process allows the mind to stabilize in the middle ground, the place where consciousness resides.

The Correlation Between the Mind & the Blockage

In the dissolving process, how is it that your mind connects and then dissolves the tension or blockage in your body, despite the density or subtlety of that blockage?

We might even ask, how can you deliberately connect, become aware of, and *feel* the blockages within the physical body with your mind only? People with normal nerves will feel pain if you hit them forcefully on a sensitive body part. It's also true too, that sometime later, they can feel the energetic blockages inside their physical body as a throbbing-type pain. This is an energy block.

Similarly, too, a person can be erotically stimulated in a sensitive spot and feel the utmost pleasure. In powerful emotional situations, like that of falling in love, grief, or being frustrated with situations where you lack control, you can consciously feel your emotions, whether they are positive or negative. In Taoism, with a concentration of mind effort, you can increase, decrease, or decrease your physical pain, pleasure, and/or emotions. So yes, you can feel what happens inside your physical body with your mind.

With relation to externally induced situations, the mind concentrates on them instead of diffusing. The individual's attention is drawn to it, whether it's pain, pleasure, or any other emotion. Here, the awareness is directed at this object of what's occurring. An agenda, we might say.

Essentially, this requires that the mind be focused, not distracted, nor scattered in any way. You can divert the mind to focus as an intention. And so, in dissolving a blockage, your recognition or interpretation of what the individual is observing, along with the feelings, affects the individual, as the "you" or as the "observer."

By going deeper and more fully inside the blockage towards its source, the mind moves further away from the original point of contact with the blockage. This method takes some practice, but its rewards are great and long-lasting. Emotional and physical pain blockages can be lessened, removed, and broken through. Here, the mind is all-powerful, in fact. And that saying which says, "Mind over matter" is poignant within this methodology as a Taoist practice.

Purposeful Sexual Meditation

Since the dawn of time, a plethora of beliefs has always existed concerning the meanings and permissible rules of sexual engagement in modern society. At one end of the scale, sex is seen as a nasty act, bordering on evil and being something to avoid if one is to gain purity. Or perhaps even something to be engaged in as little as possible, or only according to the rules of a certain belief set or religion.

At the other end of the scale, consensual sex between a man and a woman can also be viewed as a healthy, purposeful, human activity and as a celebration of the life force that we have been given by God.

We could conclude, therefore, that sex has the potential to be either a blissful or a bad deed, depending on the opinions and openness of the participants taking part. Western culture often dictates all sorts of meanings to vanilla, consensual sex, but Taoists believe that sex is just another chi or meditation practice. It's not considered to be non-spiritual in any religious or philosophical sense.

The practice of how you use Taoist meditation is basically the same here, regardless of the mode of engagement. So, you may meditate while you are standing, sitting, moving, lying down, or engaging in exercise practices. Here, the same inner and outer dissolving techniques can be used too.

Why Meditate During Sex?

While enjoying sexual activity, most people become more active to where the energy of the physical body becomes flush, and where the mind and emotions soar to heightened levels. For many people, it's easier to feel and influence the body's energies, as well as the physical tissues during play or intercourse than at any other time. Sex can let out the procreative force, which also unleashes creativity and awareness.

It's also important to note that much of the population will always find it more comfortable to access the chi via solo, meditative means, rather than through the symbiotic method of sexual meditation with another. It is necessary to mention sex as a meditation means, however.

It's via passionate sex that innate physical and psychic capacities can become accessible far more naturally though. Additionally, for many, the sexual act naturally enhances their awareness of chi sensations too. It's truly possible to keep one's awareness open while making love, and an individual can begin to feel the different kinds of physical and energetic blockages inside of their system. Learning to direct internal energy generated from lovemaking into an injured or diseased part of the body can, in fact, dissolve, break through, or even heal it.

The Power of Sexual Union

It's true too, that an individual can also direct the partner's sexual energy to loop into their own blockages to aid in dissolving them. Similarly, the partner can direct their energy towards helping a particular problem.

It's said to be possible to mutually dissolve any blocked energy that happens to exist in either party's bodies, according to the Taoist belief system. Interestingly too, Dr. Stephen Chang explored this within his title The *Tao of Sexology: The Book of Infinite Wisdom*, where he outlines certain sexual positions for healing. There are positions mentioned which serve the purposes of the woman to aid in her healing, and positions which help to heal the man, too. This book will be added to the *Suggested Reading* list at the end of this title.

The core of purposeful sexual meditation involves adapting the Taoist meditation dissolving process into the process of making love with a partner. The individuals link their consciousness' to one another, and then the mind can go within his or her mind-stream for the purposes of dissolving any blockages in the linked energetic system, the one that's created both energetically and physically.

Coming into connection with the consciousness of another is thoroughly explored throughout the process of making love. Taoists believe it takes much more skill, psychic power, and adaptation to gain such contact with another person when separate, as opposed to utilizing meditative sex. The reason given is that during sexual involvement, the partners' energy is not only heightened but immediate.

The Achievement of Inner Alchemy

There were 2 major forms of alchemy in ancient China. That of external alchemy and that of internal alchemy. In the case of external alchemy, also practiced in medieval Europe and the Middle East, we tend to conjure up images of a sage, a witch, or a wizard. And when internal alchemy is proposed, most people don't know what picture to conjure up at all. Many people may dredge up an image of a master sitting cross-legged in a cave, perhaps working on some type of enlightenment. Others might envision mystical charts with symbols of energy centers, chakras, or other types of energy channels surrounded in mysticism.

In the modern world of Taoism, people are practicing internal alchemy, but this isn't only in caves and monasteries, but also within their own homes and communities. Many enjoy the same concepts of the internal alchemists of ancient times. Whereby, they learn to transmute, change, transfigure, stabilize, and continue as a daily practice.

The Achievement of External Alchemy

External achievers of alchemy seek to create, distill, and magically transmute physical substances, by using herbs, minerals, and metals. Their costly lab experiments are aimed at creating a physical substance some might call the "philosopher's stone," which, when ingested, might cure any disease, reverse the aging process and even allow for physical immortality. The external alchemists are part of a bigger, more mystical tradition, however.

In ancient times, internal and external alchemists were known to be wise men with highly developed souls.

Internal Alchemy

Internal alchemy utilizes the human body, the mind, and the consciousness. In essence, internal alchemists practice the equivalent of changing lead into gold by changing things like foolishness into wisdom, greed into generosity, anger into compassion, fear into acceptance, and so on. They aren't looking for physical immortality as much as the complete freedom for the consciousness (or the soul). Sometimes internal alchemy may mean different things in various Taoist practices and applications. However, the common bond is a series of transformations which take place over time.

The way of Taoist internal alchemy is that the alchemical part comes prior to progress. And in this way, living via Tao by means of a series of transformations occurs. The aim is body to chi, chi to spirit, spirit to emptiness, emptiness to Tao.

There are many ways to allow for these transformations. Most are difficult to ascertain by way of writing. And this is because they must be taught by a living adept. A universal technique, however, is the dissolving practice with specific methodologies for each of the 8 energy bodies. We'll take a look at the 8 energy bodies very soon.

Taoist Meditation Practices & Setting Your Intention

Utilizing any type of Taoist spiritual work is practiced for 3 primary reasons. Taoist meditation is designed for each level. You must decide where you'd like to move to with any given meditation.

1. The need to cope with the ever-increasing pressures of the modern age, including the stresses on our physical, emotional, and mental health. The resolution can help us energize, heal, and relax the body as it's slowed down, by making it quiet, and releasing the tensions within the mind.

2. The innate desire to connect directly and deeply personally to the source of spirituality that is greater than our limited personality and ego. This source is known as the spirit or soul, and what the Taoists refer to as "being." The resolution to this need is found in the Taoist meditation practices where you learn to dissolve and resolve the spiritual, emotional, and psychic conflicts that prevent your mind and spirit from becoming still. Inner peace can be achieved here.

3. The spiritual desire to transform your inner world until your individuality merges with the unchanging source of the universe. To God, spirit, a higher power, universal consciousness, and Tao. The resolution is a stage of meditation, and it requires an open-ended commitment for as much time as it takes, be it weeks, months, years, decades, or (in many cases) an entire lifetime.

So where should you go? It starts with a knowing or what some say is a calling within oneself. Do what you can do for right now, this very minute. You'll only have success with what you can stand to do, or that with which you might grow to love to do. Otherwise, meditation will become stagnant, unenjoyable, and a chore.

Stress and tension can build up and compound over days, weeks, months, and years. Many people feel tired and drained because their body doesn't get enough of what it needs to properly repair, relax, and rest. And so, unfortunately, many operate below their capacity. And, although there are many benefits to maintaining an active lifestyle, most exercise systems focus on developing the muscles only, and can be ridiculously harsh and demanding. Inner exercise can be something far more vital, and Taoists believe that you can heal and empower yourself from the inside out!

It's true that in both Western and Eastern medicine, the state of your internal organs is what determines your overall health. So, from the perspective of Chinese medicine, all exercise should be focused on clearing, strengthening, and progressing any type of healing from the inside out. Since Chinese medical theory also considers the organs as the governors of the emotions, they are directly and intimately connected to how much energy or vitality you can express in general.

But how do you exercise your internal organs? And how do you build up and grow your energy so that you can promote both healing and strength? Let's move to our next section and see what can be done.

Heaven & Earth: A Healing Qigong

Heaven and Earth Qigong is a 3000-year-old system of exercise that's made to clear out any kind of stagnant energy within an individual. It can heal body imbalances, release stuck tissues, negative emotions, and also accelerate an individual's ability to focus, including mental processing. It's a two-part movement.

Even people who are new to the Qigong techniques can learn the Heaven and Earth form with minimal time investment. They might start feeling the results of training right from the get-go.

For truly dedicated students, Heaven and Earth's many threads are activated and integrated in a way that offers a taste of what's possible from the deeper study of the Taoist arts. Heaven and Earth is a favorite amongst beginning students and more dedicated students.

Heaven and Earth takes the idea from "Dragon" and "Tiger," and from "Energy Gates'" foundational Qigong sets. Heaven and Earth contains everything within them, but also builds upon them by gently opening, stretching, and also releasing tightness and stuck energies within the body's soft tissues. It does this while progressively tuning the individual into the subtleties of qi. Additionally, Heaven and Earth is a two-part exercise, rather than a set of 5, 6, or more movements. Here, its simplistic format encourages the internal focus needed to train deeper, more sophisticated internal energy techniques.

Developing Qi with One Movement

As with most Qigong systems, generally the aim is to develop an aspect, layer or neigong thread in just one move. After this, the focus on different and/or deeper content occurs in the next move. In this way, the qi generated in the prior move is passed up to the next, but only if it's performed correctly.

It's true too, that most internal exercises are designed to enhance qi circulation throughout a series of coordinated moves. And when placed together, they form a set. "Gods," "Energy Gates," "Dragon," "Tiger," Tai Chi, and Bagua all basically operate in this way, but to varying degrees. Each is made to generate qi and achieve and grow resiliency and vitality. However, Heaven and Earth Qigong is somewhat different. Let's see why…

With only one continuous motion being utilized, the emphasis is truly upon building layer upon layer of internal content through the scope of many repetitions. This occurs instead of variations of movement sequences. As you develop the quality of motion at each stage, energy enhancement naturally follows. Here, each layer of whichever neigong thread you are focused on must be engaged, activated, and perfected before adding the next. Additionally, you'll need a certain degree of perfection at each layer before progressing further, or you'll simply revert to struggling with the layers rather than integrating them.

In every Heaven and Earth session, you'll repeat each individual layer several (or more) times. This is so you might bring alive any given aspect of neigong and then stabilize it within the other layers you've already perfected. Next, and when focusing upon the next layer, you'll have the possibility of integrating that thread into your form. If any layer is intermittent or just outside of your ability to stabilize it, spend additional time at that stage, and don't be too quick to add more until you feel satisfied with where you are.

Exponential Energy Growth is Key

The main or key 'ingredient' behind exponential energy growth occurs in Heaven and Earth's specialized makeup, which was made to engage everything in the physical body and its energy, from the etheric field to the central channel, and all the layers in between. In terms of mastering the progression, Heaven and Earth is the first 'water tradition' neigong to work at this pivotal depth, developing the physical content and developing the foundation necessary for ongoing success.

Heaven and Earth's Range of Energetic & Internal Layers

- Alignments
- Bending
- Stretching
- Twisting
- Wrapping
- Opening
- Closing
- Pulsing
- Lengthening

- Flowing
- Breathing
- Technique building
- Ethereal field work
- Feeling
- Moving
- Transforming
- Macrocosmic orbits
- Microcosmic orbits
- Outer Dissolving
- Techniques for the left and right channels of energy
- Techniques for the central channel of energy
- Techniques for the internal organs
- Techniques for the lower tantien

In essence, the real effort is in developing your ability to integrate all the skills listed. Practice, practice, practice makes perfect. And you can fine tune your skillset and continue as you layer the actioning energetically, and in turn, deepen your embodiment of neigong.

Taoist Breathing as a Necessity

Qigong breathing is based on Taoist breathing methods that focus on returning the way we breathe to what is said to be in harmony with nature. This methodology focuses upon creating a circular breath that starts from the belly and is very relaxed. These methods can be practiced either sitting or standing.

The Taoist expression of how energy moves in humans comes primarily from the 16 components of neigong, or what's known as the internal energy system. Breathing plays a primary role in the system, and it's the true foundation for all of the other neigong components. It's also the first neigong component.

Frozen Diaphragm Breathing & Locating the Cause of a Poor Breathing Technique

The simple fact is most humans don't breathe well. There are countless studies on the effects of poor breathing for your health. When a person doesn't breathe well, it actually contracts their body and creates unnecessary tension and stress within it. This means that learning to breathe well is key.

Breathing from the Heels is a Wise Man's Breath

Correct breathing is at the heart of Taoist arts and other Eastern practices, too. This includes different forms of yoga and Buddhist meditation. Breathing well is the way to good health, lessened stress, and a key part of Taoism. "Breathing from the heels" is an expression used to invoke proper breath. It also incorporates the entire bottom section of the body, as if the breath is circulating further. Remember, the entire body must become oxygenated, so this way of breath has a methodology to it.

The Taoist 8 Energy Body Theory

The 8 Energy Bodies:

- The flesh of the physical body
- The chi body, which energizes the physical body
- The emotional body, which gives energy to your emotions, both positive and negative
- The mental body, which causes thoughts to occur, whether with clarity or by way of confusion
- The psychic body, which allows us to find our hidden internal selves and aids our intuition, or psychic perceptions become concrete
- The causal body, which causes karma to flow
- The body of individuality, which enables the actual ignition of the full spiritual self (or essence)
- The realization of Tao or the entire cosmos, which few people ever actualize within their lifetime

The ancient masters who devised these exercises more than 6000 years ago were very practical people. In truth, if something worked, they used it; if it didn't, it was discarded from the repertoire altogether. In general, internal exercises are designed to energize the entire body, to balance out energy, and to promote effective functioning of the internal organs. There are exercises for many common ailments such as the common cold, headaches, heart disease, cancer, and arthritis, as examples. Learning how to balance health in accordance with the natural laws is amazing and promotes longevity, too. In fact, Eastern practices like Taoism have been enjoying these methods for thousands of years.

Some of the exercises which you might like to practice, and which are mentioned in Dr. Chang's title called *The Complete System of Self-Healing: Internal Exercises* are mentioned below. This title will be added to the *Suggested Reading* list at the end of this title.

Healing Exercises (Internals):

- Deer
- Crane
- Heavenly drum
- Nerve exercises
- 5 animal exercises
- Stomach exercise
- Heart exercise
- Liver exercise
- Kidney exercise

These exercises (and more) are thoroughly explained within Dr. Chang's above-mentioned text, and they can be used singularly (or in sets) to alleviate conditions and diseases, and to accelerate health and aid in longevity.

In the next chapter, we'll be discussing the importance of the Taoist diet and practices related to this methodology. And, in this way, the practitioner can learn about balancing health through the aid of dietary incorporations and as a pivotal understanding. Health as it relates to diet can be life-changing, and it's a game changer for many who suffer from illness, disease, or conditions they can't seem to move away from.

Chapter 6: The Taoism Diet for Energy & Longevity

To truly comprehend the Taoist diet, you'll have to first understand more about Taoist beliefs. As we know, Taoism comes from the core of East Asian and Chinese culture and has roots as deep as 2,000 years or more, although it's only spread to the West in more recent times as people begin to reject materialism for deeper spiritual methodology and practices.

Taoists are egoless and mostly humble people that emphasize true compassion, balance, moderation, and humility, which is stressed through their minimalistic eating habits, too.

Although not known for their rule breaking because of their caring and non-active viewpoints, Taoism focuses upon the human connection with relation to nature, and they don't believe in the rigid and orderly ways of modern society, preferring to follow the natural flow of the cosmos. The common Taoist terminology from the yin and yang belief system refers to the positive and negative energies within the universe.

The five colors blind eyes.

The five tones deafen ears.

The five tastes blur tongues.

Fast horses and breathtaking hunts make minds wild and crazy.

Things rare and expensive make people lose their way.

That's why a sage tends to the belly, not the eye, always ignores that and chooses this.

- **Excerpt from the Tao Te Ching, Part 12**

In ancient times, the Taoist diet consisted of mainly fresh fruits and vegetables, with little meat and no grain. During more contemporary times, the diet has changed to being mostly based around the acceptance of whole grains, as well as the fresh fruits and vegetables of traditional times. Some Taoists still adhere to the older belief systems, however, especially by way of their non-consumption of grains.

Taoism is all about everything natural, and humans are a part of that nature. One of the most important beliefs is to eat only real food, meaning that we should always avoid unnatural and manmade substances that the body cannot process, or which may contain unbalanced flavors, like artificial additives, colors, numbers, etc. Heavily processed foods that contain little or no nutritional value, like white flour, sugar and fast or processed foods are also considered to be inedible. These are not things that the body is designed to consume, and they don't grow from the earth, so are not really natural foods which are fit for human consumption.

In much of the historical Taoist literature, a lot of mention is made of the sages or men of old, including people who existed in pre-history. And some of the texts talk about them existing only on breath, and not consuming any food at all. They lived as they were born and only gained nutrients from the qi or yin and yang from the universe. This practice was known as "Bigu" and is sometimes utilized within some of the Taoist hermit traditions and mythological ideas, but it's not something that's practical or even safe for modern people, for obvious reasons. Taoists believe that the human state has altered a lot since the ancient times, and the ancient state has since fallen, meaning that it's perfectly acceptable to eat foods nowadays.

The most ancient Taoists are believed to have had a diet that reflected upon a notion of sagacious deeds and enlightenment, and they also stemmed from before the development of agriculture. Therefore, in the earliest traditions, grains were not to be consumed by Taoists at all. There weren't actually any available via farming methods, and so they weren't consumed. Other reasons are said to be because of other health concerns, because of a reverence for some mythological, non-agricultural cultural stances, and perhaps other social factors, too. The minimalist approach was often used to explain it, stating that Taoists live off more than food alone and subconsciously gain energy from the cosmos. At this point, it's also important to note that the main reason provided in many of the early texts for not eating grain was to not arouse the '3 worms.'

The 3 Worms

The earliest mythological explanation for abstaining from grain is the 3 worms. These are said to be literal, being 3 demonic worms that were able to live in the intestines of human beings. These 3 worms were responsible for the decomposition of the physical body after death.

Of course, additionally, and as their goal is to devour the physical body, it's in their best interest that they make individuals pass away as quickly as is possible. Before passing away, it's said that the 3 worms would live in a person's intestines, feeding off the rotten bio-matter being digested there. Additionally, as the intestines digested the grain, the 3 worms would eat the waste that was produced from this process. And as they fed on the grains, they would grow stronger and stronger, and later be able to feed on the rest of the body too, thus causing the individual to pass away far more quickly.

As we know, longevity for continued cultivation is one of the primary goals of many Taoists, and the object of the diet was originally to stave off the 3 worms by lowering (or not including) intake of grain.

From a modern perspective, it could be that the earliest Taoists simply noted a correlation between caloric intake, and aging, or ill health with relation to grain. Assuming that a cell has an infinite number of possible divisions during its lifecycle, it would be necessary to dramatically slow down the metabolic process in order to stave the process of cell division. Another possible explanation is just the reference for a pre-civilized or pre-agricultural period of time, where men neither farmed nor engaged in the social action of a surplus food-producing culture.

It's also important for many Taoists that vegetables are eaten in the right seasons, and that they're either steamed or stir fried when prepared. Boiling is said to take out the natural goodness where the water takes the nutrients and not the food.

Fruits tend to be dried or baked, and eating tropical fruits is frowned upon as being unbalancing to the five tastes (which will be mentioned soon) due to their strong; often citric tastes. Being free of any manmade intervention is also key with any food types.

Generally speaking, red and blue meats, including pork, rabbit, snails, etc., should be avoided at all costs. Poultry and game birds are not frowned upon, and neither is fish. However, fish and other seafood should only be eaten once a week because of their high yin quantity. Some fish, like salmon, mackerel, shark, and swordfish, which are highly yin based, should be altogether avoided.

Consuming alcohol, caffeine, or chewing/smoking tobacco is frowned upon because of their refined nature. The modern Taoist relies on moderation in their eating habits and must try to avoid consuming anything too pungent, or in large amounts. Other examples are garlic, onions, ginger, etc. Preservatives are not to be used at all.

Comparing Taoist And Modern Western Diets

In the West, the lifestyle and dietary habits have contributed to the dramatic rise in problems such as cancer, stress, heart disease, obesity, diabetes, arthritis and more.

The emphasis has moved away from the initial prevention methodology (by eating naturally and healthily) and unfortunately moved towards drugs and other fixes after the person has become unwell.

Taoists believe that what is of primary importance is natural health, not doctors and their drug-filled medicines or fixes, and this can best be achieved through eating the more natural foods. Remember too, that the body regenerates itself, and even the skin tissue and organs take about 2 to 3 years per cycle, and the bones are replaced after 7 years, and all this occurring from what goes into your mouth.

Nature can do its work when given the right tools to work with. Primarily, natural foods which have been grown organically without the use of artificial fertilizers, chemicals, or pesticides are key.

The Taoist Diet as a Contrast to the Modern Western Diet is:

- Low in fat
- High in energy
- Vitamin and mineral based
- Easy for the body to digest
- Unrefined and unprocessed
- Highly nutritious
- Simple to prepare

This means daily Western items (like milk and bread) are considered almost toxic to strict Taoists. Instead, rice and soya milk are used, with skimmed milk generally being accepted for many modern followers.

The Approach from the Ground Up

Qigong

The Taoist exercises used to maintain and move with the qi (energy of the universe) is used in conjunction with diet.

Methods include meditation and focused physical movements which are used to balance the energy both within and around the physical body. This helps to maintain both physical and mental health.

Generally, the energy is drawn from the earth, and then upward. Similarly, the concept known as "rooting" is the basis of Tai Chi and many of the Chinese and Taoist martial arts types, too. Therefore, the Taoist context of power, being from the ground up was thought of as the best way to get vital energy from food.

Just like Taoist Qigong, the Taoist diet also stresses a 'ground up' approach to the consumption of vegetables. That is, that plants should be consumed in high percentage of total diet, especially those found below the ground (like root vegetables), as opposed to those higher up on tress, e.g. oranges and apples, as examples.

It's said that earth-bound vegetables have more energy too, and the ability to deliver more qi to the body. Yams, potatoes, root crops, carrots, and turnips were thought to deliver good earth energy, which helped the spleen (a major part of the immune system functioning) to become stronger, and more therefore more rooted.

"With all the conflicting information about diet we get nowadays, it can leave one confused as to what steps to take in order to be as healthy as possible. The problem with most of the nutrition advice today, is that it tends to look at foods and macro/micronutrients in isolation, which is typical of the Western reductionist perspective. Therefore, in order to understand diet from a holistic point of view, we must look to more established systems of medicine that were developed long before this reductionist mentality took hold. The ancient (and modern) Taoist masters have always recognized the complexity and holistic nature of the human mind-body-spirit triad and developed a system for eating and living that honored and supported this natural way of being. In fact, the Taoists honed this system to the point where those who closely followed its tenets and guidelines regularly lived well beyond 100 years old and furthermore, did so with amazing vigor, mental clarity, agility and overall health.

Many of the suggestions the Taoists offer for a healthy, whole lifestyle will remind you of things you may have heard from other modern sources. Science is just now confirming what the Taoists always knew."

Excerpt from *Taoist Long-Life Diet* - **Lee Style**

Some Basic Dietary Principles

Nature

Taoism is a philosophy of nature *and* a religion. Millions of years of evolution have shaped humans to be what they are, and throughout this time, humans have evolved by eating natural foods. It's only relatively recently that diet has changed so much to include so many artificial foods. There is more processed food, additives, chemicals, flavors, and toxins nowadays. In truth, the more of these in the diet there are, the more difficult it is for the organism to cope and adapt.

Processed foods may have had most of the natural goodness, vitamins, fibre, and minerals removed during the processing stage/s, and they may have been stored in tins or packets for some months, or even longer than that, so that they're no longer fresh and wholesome to eat.

Additionally, avoiding tobacco, alcohol, coffee, tea, sugar, drugs, desserts, and other artificial stimulants is also highly recommended, and this is because they contain toxins which might clog up the body and put a strain on the organs, as well as that they're unnatural stimulants which can burden the body's natural processes. They're not balanced foods either; this is because they may appear to provide energy, but truthfully, they're really only stimulating the body to use up some of its own natural reserves. In addition, they don't contain balanced amounts of protein, vitamins, or minerals which the body needs as well as energy.

In the Western lifestyle, dietary habits have contributed to the huge rise in such problems as heart disease, obesity, stress, cancer, arthritis etc. The emphasis has moved away from prevention and towards drugs and being fixed (after the fact), very unfortunately. There are some simple guidelines we can do. What is of primary importance is health, and not doctors and medicines.

Taoists believe that their good health can best be achieved through eating natural foods and via other Taoist practices. Remember too, that the body regenerates itself, and nature can do its work well, but only if given the right tools to do so. Ideally, natural foods have been grown organically without the use of artificial fertilizers, chemicals, or pesticides. It's important that we give our bodies great 'fuel' so that we can live healthier and live for as long as possible.

Environment

Each individual generally becomes adapted to the climate or locality with which they live, and so foods that are eaten in a hot country may not be suitable for a colder climate, and vice versa.

It's always advisable to eat food that is grown locally and in season, too. Food that comes from a distance may not be as fresh and might have been stored for a longer time, but primarily is probably out of season. If you eat summer-type foods in the wintertime, then you're tricking your body into thinking its summertime and not giving it what matches for the season at hand. Additionally, food from a long distance creates more pollution for the environment because it must travel further to get to your locality.

Eating in tune with the environment also means timing things properly. And here, the body wants to rest at night-time, so don't eat after 8 pm as a general rule of thumb. A big breakfast is the best way forward and eating less later in the day is key. Also, avoiding drinking before meals is incredibly important, as this dilutes the digestive juices which are needed to process foods. Variety is important too. Trying to eat more root vegetables in winter and leafier ones in the summer is highly recommended.

Whole foods are also important. The B vitamins in wholemeal bread are important in dealing with stress, and the natural fibre has a cleansing effect on the digestive system, although some Taoists take a no grain approach and negate wheat altogether. This really is a personal choice.

And so, food must be found as far as possible in its natural state, but the way cooking is important, too. In a balanced diet, foods being prepared should be neither raw nor overcooked. Too much raw food creates weakness internally, due to too much *cold energy* in the center of the stomach. Weakness in the limbs may occur too, with issues like anaemia, coldness, and bad circulation which can all result from too much raw or cold food.

As modern people, we have adapted to cooked food, much unlike wild animals who don't live for as long as we do. The best method is stir-frying where the food is cooked very quickly, and the flavors are sealed in with the oil used. Steaming is also a great method, especially if the water is used in making a sauce so that none of the goodness is lost while cooking. Boiling vegetables is not a good method, however, because most of the vitamins are destroyed in the heat, or even thrown away with the cooking water used, and so this is like throwing the tea away and eating the tea leaves.

These simple rules are taken from of a few simple natural principles and become self-evident once they've been put into practice for a while. It's all about building a strong basis for health using a time-tested and more traditional approach. There's a way forward, and it's simply a matter of looking at things in a different light. So, if you're not used to this kind of dietary practice, you might need some time to adjust to a newer way of eating. As with anything you eat, there's a natural form of it somewhere, you just have to look for it a little harder. In truth, it wasn't all that long ago that all the food was natural.

Here is an excerpt from *The Taoist Art of K'ai Men* from the Chapter named "The Importance of Good Health" - **Chee Soo**

"Why do we eat? Is it because we are hungry or like the flavour of certain things, or do we eat just for the sake of eating — clock-watching in other words? Lunch is at one, tea at five, dinner at eight, and it becomes a ritual, whether we need the food or not, and whether we are hungry or not. Because of this, few people realize the importance of eating and drinking correctly, and never fully appreciate that most illnesses are caused through bad and senseless eating and drinking habits.

Eating is essential to us, of course, and the pleasure of eating is important too, but we should all understand that the whole of our life revolves around our food intake and breathing, which matter to us not only physically but also mentally and spiritually. Through correct eating habits and learning to understand what is and what is not good for us, we can ensure that the body maintains constant good health, and that we grow older without looking old or feeling or being old within ourselves. Many sages of ancient China lived to be 130 to 200 years old, which itself is a great encouragement to cultivate the correct eating habits.

Proper eating enables the bones, tissues and organs of the body to remain strong and healthy, and so ensures that the Yin and Yang are in balance within the body, and that ill health is foreign to it. For this to be the result, it is necessary to take into account not only the type of food eaten, but also when it is eaten and how it is chewed and digested.

Nowadays, most people expect to have colds and influenza in the wintertime, and, when they are beyond the age of forty or so, to suffer from various aches and pains — including, possibly, rheumatism and arthritis. This is completely the wrong attitude to take; and no one eating the Ch'ang Ming (Taoist long-life therapy) way need expect ill health at all.

Very few people also realize that, through sensible eating and drinking habits, and in some cases the added use of herbs, the majority of illnesses and diseases can be cured quite quickly and the deterioration of the body stopped in just ten to fourteen days. We are born as a part of nature and nature herself grows and cures all things.

As far back as the reign of the Yellow Emperor this was understood. The Nei Ching, which is reputed to have been written by the Yellow Emperor and to be the oldest medical book in existence, is the classic work on Chinese internal medicine, and it states that "Yin is active within and is a guardian of the Yang, whereas Yang is active on the outside and is the regulator of the Yin" — equating harmony of the Yin and Yang with health and constant youthfulness, and disharmony with ill health, disease or death.

Even our foods are either Yin or Yang, though it would take more than a lifetime to understand the subject completely, in all its details. It is, however, possible to give some general guidelines as to what should or should not be eaten, and this the rest of this chapter sets out to do. The recommendations given are based on the sort of food and drink generally consumed in the West, but this does not make them any the less valuable to those who wish to attain the depths and the full benefits of K'ai Men and the constant good health that goes with it."

Eating Recommendations for Consistent Good Health

Increase Your Consumption of These Foods to Comply with a Taoist Diet:

- Wholemeal bread
- Brown rice
- Barley
- Oats
- Buckwheat
- Rye
- Maize
- Millet
- Quinoa
- Fresh locally grown vegetables in season, organic if possible
- Beans
- Nuts
- Seeds (roasted)
- Soya bean curd (tofu)
- Chicken
- Turkey
- Eggs
- Non-fatty white fish or seafood
- Prawns
- Soya milk
- Rice milk
- Skimmed milk
- Soya yogurt

- Low fat yogurt
- Low fat vegetarian cheese
- Seaweed
- Nori
- Kelp
- Natural soya sauce
- Dates
- Sultanas
- Raisins
- Figs
- Apples
- Strawberries
- Sea salt only, in strict moderation
- Herbs
- Herbal teas and coffees,
- China tea; green or black
- Honey, in moderation

Reduce your Intake of These Foods to Comply with a Taoism Diet:

- White bread
- White flour
- White rice
- Tinned and packet foods
- Chemical additives
- Colors
- Preservatives
- Flavourings

- Fruit acids
- Red meat
- Beef
- Pork
- Veal
- Lamb
- Bacon
- Sausages
- Meat products or extracts
- Red or blue fish
- Poultry or fish which is high in fat (duck, goose, haddock)
- Boiled, fried, or poached eggs
- Full fat milk
- Cheese
- Butter
- Lard
- Dripping
- Alcohol
- Tobacco
- Coffee
- Sugar
- Drugs
- Artificial vitamins, supplements etc.
- Mustard
- Rock salt
- Rhubarb
- Spinach (high in oxalic acid)

- Ice-cold food, like ice cream
- Cream
- Sodas
- Raw and uncooked food
- Fresh fruit which is out of season or imported from a different climate
- Tropical fruit drinks
- Deep fried food

A balanced diet in Taoism is considered one of the 8 pillars, taken from the symbolism given as the 8 trigrams in the Pa-Kua symbolism within Taoism.

Although many true Taoist teachings have been kept a secret for centuries, it's important to note that the 8 pillars are what true Taoists adhere to.

The 8 Pillars:

1. The Tao of philosophy
2. The Tao of revitalisation (internal exercises)
3. The Tao of a balanced diet
4. The Tao of sexual wisdom
5. The Tao of healing arts
6. The Tao of mastery
7. The Tao of success

8. The Tao of forgotten foods

With relation to the Tao of forgotten foods, there are many herbs which have been shown to alleviate, cure, and help with longevity, generally speaking. In fact, true Taoists believe that foods which come from the supermarket are the lowest kinds of foods, and that these foods are the foods without strength. They believe this is so because God created a multitude of wonderful foods from branches and leaves, and also from roots which are excellent for human consumption. These foods are known as the "forgotten foods" and were used by the ancients who knew the strength and capacity of them for health and wellbeing maintenance. Some examples of forgotten foods include ginseng, ginger, cinnamon, astragalus, bitter almond, zingiber, licorice, and acorus.

The forgotten foods and herbs can give everlasting strength, compared to foods which we might call "regular," and these regular foods give only temporary strength. There are also cleansing and purifying qualities within the forgotten foods and herbs which allow them to remain on shelves for years, without rotting, and which have great benefits which can last for years.

In this chapter, we'll focus primarily on the diet which relates to whole foods, and the foods with which we come into contact with every day. In this system of understanding, we will learn about balance and also about the five-taste theory.

The Five-Taste Theory

The five-taste theory is remarkable because it allows humans to understand the five categories of foods which relate to the organs, superficial organs, and the openings of the body, and how balance can be maintained through purposeful eating.

Each taste relates to a specific element, organ, superficial organ, and organ opening, and you might really have a true "aha" moment once you get more familiar with this practice. Let's take a look at these now.

The element of *metal* is associated with the taste known as *spicy*. Spicy foods affect the lungs, large intestines, skin, and nose.

The element of *wood* is associated with the taste known as *sour*. Sour foods affect the liver, gallbladder, nerves, and eyes.

The element of *earth* is associated with the taste known as *sweet*. Sweet foods affect the spleen, pancreas, stomach, muscles, and mouth.

The element of *water* is associated with the taste known as *salty*. Salty foods affect the kidneys and bladder, bones, and ears.

The element of *fire* is associated with the taste known as *bitter*. Bitter foods affect the heart, small intestine, blood vessels, and tongue.

As an example, we might say that spicy food is excellent for the large intestines and the lungs. We're already familiar with curry, cinnamon, and chilli being good for certain types of coughs and colds, even in the Western world. In fact, these have been used for many centuries as home remedies for these types of illnesses. The other categories are also wonderful for each of the organ areas, superficial organs, and organ openings as already described above. Another example is: salty foods being recommended for the good health of the kidneys. However, an over balance of salty foods would harm the kidneys and might even cause water retention and overstimulation.

A further example might be bitter foods being fantastic for the heart. An under use of bitter foods can affect the heart's performance, generally speaking, and an overuse of foods recommended for the heart may cause it to beat too fast, so that it's being overused.

Primarily, we can understand that the dietary requirements of an individual are all about balance, and when there is balance, there is harmony.

The recommended amount of foods per day is broken down into percentages. Salty foods 20%; bitter foods 20%; spicy foods; sour foods 20%; and sweet foods 20%, as a daily recommendation for balance overall.

The most interesting part of the five-taste theory is how the elements can generate or destroy one another. Metal enhances water. Water enhances wood. Wood enhances fire. Fire enhances earth. Earth enhances metal.

The destructive cycle is as follows: metal destroys and dominates wood. Wood destroys and dominates earth. Earth destroys and dominates water. Water destroys and dominates fire. Fire destroys and dominates metal.

Using regulation within food consumption can stop the unbalanced equilibrium which can cause illness and disease from imbalance. We might say that a Taoism diet can compensate for the destructive and dominating cycles.

Someone with weak kidneys may be eating too much salt (water element) and be surprised that their intake of spicy (metal element) foods isn't enough, therefore increasing spicy foods so that the ratio is 20% along with the other tastes in equal proportions. This can be extremely helpful. Additionally, metal feeds water, and here, the elements are in their regulating cycle, not their destructive cycle. The kidney is associated with the water element, and this element is fed by metal. The metal element is associated with spicy foods which increases the capacity of the lung and large intestine, and therefore increases and strengthens the kidneys. By way of understanding this methodology, it will remove the susceptibility of the weakness in the kidneys, as shown by this example. In this way, we can use any of the elements and their direct qualities to enhance certain organs, superficial organs, and openings of the body. The golden rule is the (20:20:20:20:20) ratio for each of the five tastes.

Let's do another example for the heart (which is represented by fire) and is of the bitter taste. Fire is enhanced by wood, so we can enhance the heart by eating foods related to both fire and wood. Wood uses the taste of sour. In our next section, we will list some of the foods represented in each category.

Sweet Foods Examples:

Oatmeal, milk, lettuce, beans, kale, ice cream, honey, eggplant, cucumber, corn, cream, dried fruit, coconut, carrots, candy, cakes, canned fruits, Brazil nuts, almonds, beans, bran, wheat, walnuts, sweet potatoes, peanuts, peas, rice, squash, sugar, sunflower seeds, sweet and fruit, pecans, soda.

Sour Foods Examples:

Beef, yoghurt, barbecue sauce, turkey, vinegar, tomatoes, sprouts, sausages, sour cream, salad dressing, salami, bread, chicken, freshwater fish, liver, raw fruit, fruit juices, mayonnaise, red meats, pickles.

Bitter Foods Examples:

Green vegetables, artichokes, asparagus, tea, turnips, bamboo shoots, bok choy, cocoa, coffee, gelatin, green vegetables, heart (any animal), leeks, mushrooms, broccoli, cauliflower, celery, avocados, bitter melon.

Salty Foods Examples:

Bones, prepared beef, canned foods, cheese, egg, salt-water fish, butter, frozen foods, tofu, shellfish, seaweed, most processed foods, margarine, pickled olives, kidneys (any animal), caviar.

Spicy Foods Examples:

Wine, basil, cayenne pepper, chilli, garlic, curry, dill, ginger, lung (any animal), garlic, mustard, mint, rhubarb, pepper, parsley, oregano, onions, mustard, time, truffles, aniseed.

The maintenance of the five-taste theory means that, within a 24-hour period of time, the individual's food intake should be at a ratio of 20% per taste as discussed above. Some of the ramifications of not doing so will be discussed now.

A dietary imbalance can create illness, and from there, serious health problems may develop. The overly sweet diet may cause water retention, constipation, diabetes, indigestion, and heartburn. This is where the intake of sweets is over proportionate to the other tastes.

A primarily salty diet may induce kidney weakness, heart issues, and may even bring about issues associated with heart disease. The reason for maintaining balance as a ratio set (per 24-hour period) is so that we maintain the organs, the superficial organs, and the openings of the physical body. This is done with relation to the five elements.

As we give a 20% dietary proportional rate to the elements of metal, water, wood, fire, earth, and the coinciding tastes associated with these elements, we allow the generating cycle rather than the destructive and dominant cycle to occur. In this way, an individual may maintain true balance which applies to the various organs, superficial organs, and to the organ openings more fully. And by indirectly removing the cause of issues and illness through diet maintenance, and individual can have proper functioning if the theory is kept long term.

In Western culture, unfortunately nutrition plays a neglectful part (in most instances) with relation to health. The Eastern philosophy may help to alleviate and even cure (in some cases) conditions which have been neglected and ignored for many years.

The Golden Rule of Meal Planning

Now that we know the ratios for each of the tastes, planning meals can be so much easier to do. In fact, you can plan weeks, months, or even more (ahead of time). Some great recipes for meals are stir fry's, casseroles, rice dishes, soups, and stews, mostly because they can take foods from each of the 5 tastes.

If you need further inspiration, Asian cooking and Mediterranean meals have some great free recipes online. In fact, any culture can probably add to the flavor of the five-taste theory, and you can add or decrease amounts as needed. Just make sure balance is maintained so that the organs, superficial organs, and the openings of the physical body are maintained within each 24-hour period.

Chapter 7: Combining Spiritualism as a Daily Practice

Taoism, as we know, is the ancient Chinese philosophy that's also classified as a religion. In fact, many people within China would define it in this way, and quite intimately so. But unlike most religions, modern philosophical Taoism doesn't ask for any specific form of belief or particular initiation, per say. Becoming a Taoist can be as simple as reading Taoist textbooks to become familiar with Taoist belief systems and practices, in fact. Certain practices might include visiting temples, observing feng shui, and meditating too, as these are considered to be Taoist in nature. You can become a Taoist by observing these practices to start with. And when ready, you may begin practicing them. Additionally, living your life according to Taoist beliefs makes you a Taoist, too.

1. Read the obvious texts related to Taoism.

A great place to start is the *Tao Te Ching*. The *Tao Te Ching* (meaning, The Way and Its Power) is the original Taoist text by Lao Tzu and was published in the 3rd century. It's made up of 81 chapters and has short verses with advice on life and also speaks about the nature of the universe. Reading it and drawing your own conclusions from it, really is the first step you should take towards becoming a Taoist.

The *Tao Te Ching* teaches individuals how to connect with the universe. One of the focused principles of the *Tao Te Ching* is that there are just some things you can't understand, and that it's okay because they're a mystery. If you come across sections of the book that you can't grasp, try your best to get meaning from them, but don't get hung up on any particular philosophies or teachings, because your understanding will probably expand over time, or you will revisit them at a later date and gain a whole new understanding of them.

Some temples might even offer study groups based on the *Tao Te Ching*. If you'd enjoy studying with other people, you can look for particular study groups and attend them as you wish.

Also, read the *Chuang-tzu* which is a brilliantly organized compilation of Taoist wisdom. You can read it to be aware of the teachings, and so you might focus on changing your perspective of the world you perceive around you. It also teaches that despite the differences within the universe, the entire universe and everything within it is actually one.

2. Use other Taoist texts for meditation purposes.

There are many books that you can use to meditate on Taoist principles, and some are listed in the *Suggested Reading* list at the end of this title. Some of them will be focused on a specific type of learning and can be highly resourceful to you at different points in your life. Your local bookstore or online retailer should have a spirituality section where you can find these types of titles.

3. Focus on the premise of oneness.

The first and most intrinsic Taoist principle, is that people and nature are not separate from each other. Everything in the cosmos is actually a part of the same system or greater whole. As a Taoist, you might even focus on oneness by being more selfless, and by paying less attention to your own needs. Helping others is a part of this profound understanding, in fact. For example, you can do something like helping a charity or a community group. This can be a way to remember that people with less than you have are still connected to you, regardless of their social status, financial circumstances, race, gender, age, or culture.

4. See the exquisite balance in everything.

Just because everything in the universe is part of the same system, that doesn't mean there aren't fundamental distinctions. Taoists believe that there are 2 main distinctions, and as we know already, these can be described as being yin and yang, and these principles exist in all of nature. Dark and light, up and down, in and out, and left and right, etc. These are part of the same system because they can't exist without one another, but they are also distinctive on their own, as well.

The principle of balance can be helpful if you're struggling in any part of your life. And, according to this principle, happiness simply can't exist without sadness. Look for cyclical growth here. The principle of cyclical growth is related to balance. And in this case, the opposites balance each other out, but they don't usually occur at the same time, however. In truth, they move through cycles. So, we could say, the seasons balance one another as a great example of this.

5. Cyclical growth is key.

Cyclical growth can help you understand where your life is going. If you're experiencing any type of sadness or uncomfortableness, remind yourself that happiness will eventually show up because it's cyclical and ever-changing. It might take a while, but this sadness will eventually give way to true happiness.

6. Performing harmonious action.

Taoists believe that because seeming opposites actually balance each other out and also cycle together, you can, in fact, make one opposite from the other. A bamboo stick is a great example of this concept. During the wind, the bamboo can bend, but it doesn't break, no, not at all. By bending with the wind, the bamboo stick survives it, instead of staying straight and breaking itself in half.

As a metaphor, if you're dealing with a difficult time, accept that it will be difficult and accept your loneliness, dismay, or sadness regarding it. Embrace it for a time and know that it will pass. By doing this, you can embrace it without worry, and you won't wear yourself out by trying to be strong.

7. Join a Taoist temple if you can.

Some Taoists really enjoy going to temples for festival days. Other Taoists observe certain rites or rites dedicated to ancestors at a temple setting. Many observe festivals on behalf of local communities too. You can search for Taoist temples in your locality by performing an online search.

Each rite usually has specific stages, including offerings, purification, prayers, the singing of songs, and dancing. It really depends on what rites are being observed, though.

8. Practice the art of feng shui.

The practice of feng shui is the purposeful organization of space to create positive energy within a home or business. There are many texts related to how to use feng shui, and you can often find them at your local bookstore, or online. In fact, using feng shui is considered a Taoist practice.

9. Meditation to connect with Tao.

You might like to sit on the floor with your legs in the lotus position (your legs crossed over each other at the calf). You can also sit on the edge of a chair with your feet flat on the floor or ground (if outside). Sit with your spine upright so that it's straight and have your chin slightly pulled in. Focus on breathing through your nose from your diaphragm.

You can imagine any sickness, illness, negativity, stress, and/or pain leaving your body as you exhale. And, as you inhale, imagine a wonderful healing and relaxing light entering your body to fill it with goodness and positivity, or even healing.

Sometimes, imagining filling your lungs with air from the bottom to the top through your belly button can really help. You should always meditate in a clean and quiet space whenever possible.

    10. Practice Tai Chi.

Tai Chi is a breathing and exercise practice where you create certain body movements with inhaling and exhaling breaths. There are 5 main schools of Tai Chi, each with different types of movements and goals to reach for. But ultimately, they all focus on increasing your internal energy and effervescence from the inside out, as well as promoting the flow of external energy.

You can look for Tai Chi videos online, and this is a free way to learn the art. The best part is, you can pause the video and rewind it so you can watch it repeatedly as needed.

    11. Practice Qigong.

Qigong is a combination of both meditation practices and physical exercise that almost anyone can enjoy. Qigong includes warmup as well as awareness exercises that help individuals to meditate and connect, thereby directing the internal energy to different areas of the physical body with each move. You can practice Qigong in the privacy of your own home, or learn it by watching YouTube videos. Some gyms and temples may also offer Qigong.

Qigong directs energy to different parts of the physical body in each move. This is a little different to Tai Chi which helps you connect to both the internal and external energy.

12. Practice yoga.

The practice of yoga requires the individual to understand how the bones (yin) and the muscles and connective tissue (yang) are connected and how they can move together. Since yin and yang are a prime concept in Taoism, taking any yoga class is a form of Taoist practice.

You can learn yoga at a gym or find free classes on YouTube. Start with knowing that you can and will improve over time. Practice is key in yoga.

13. Accepting yourself.

Taoism generally teaches that the individual should live according to their own nature. By accepting yourself, including the good and bad qualities, you're actually living according to the Taoist belief system.

Accepting yourself may also mean acknowledging that (sometimes) your personality might change. Sometimes you'll be loving and kind, and sometimes you'll be angry or annoyed, as examples. Accept all aspects of your personality and realize that they're who you are.

14. Follow your instincts.

Taoism acknowledges the need for taking the time to learn about yourself as well as the world around you. The more you do this, the better your intuition will be developed. From here, you're able to listen to it. If something feels wrong, don't do it. If something feels like a good idea, go for it, and wholeheartedly so.

15. Allow for new experiences.

Being open to life and living it through experiences is a big part of the Taoism belief system. This also means being open to new experiences as they arrive in your life. Go and have a cultural experience or explore a new location from time to time.

16. Embracing quiet time.

Sometimes, technology and the 24-hour grind of life can feel truly overwhelming. Practicing Taoism means taking time to unplug from social media, the news media, and online in general, and just sitting in silence and observing the world around you. Sit outside, on your porch, or in a restaurant, or in your favorite place, and just be present. Let the mind allow you to just be.

17. Practice Taoism in the ways that make sense to you.

Every individual that practices Taoism practices it in a different way. If you like to do Tai Chi, do that. If you prefer meditation or reading purpose-filled texts, you can do that too. It's up to you how you incorporate your own daily practice. Taoism doesn't have a set belief or even a must-do practice system, so there's no wrong way to be a follower of Taoism.

18. Follow a Taoist diet.

The more classical Taoist teachings suggest that individuals avoid certain things in their diets. Abstaining from alcohol, meat (for some), beans, and grains. You don't have to follow this diet to be a Taoist, but it's similar to following the most ancient Taoist teachings if that suits your needs.

19. Physical practices.

There's no real or specific division between body and soul, but Taoism recognizes that physical actions do have a spiritual effect. Being aware of this is a great understanding in itself.

20. Maintaining purity.

In essence, Taoist texts teach the importance of keeping the body pure in order to allow an individual's spiritual health to continue. To remain in purity, an individual can avoid certain activities and foods. These include greed, envy, lust, pride, and dishonesty. And these are examples of things that should be avoided.

21. Breath work.

Breath is the most easily allowable form of chi, and there are many Taoist breathing exercises that can be followed. Taoist breathing exercises are essentially known as Qigong.

22. Ensuring energy flow.

The flow of life (or energy chi) within the physical body can be enhanced, regulated, and balanced by various forms of exercise, meditation, and techniques like acupuncture.

23. Martial arts.

Tai Chi was actually derived from Taoist exercises created by Chang San-Feng (Zhang Sanfeng) in 1127-1279 CE. The more modern forms of Tai Chi are more likely to be secular exercises than Taoist practices, however.

24. Diet Incorporation

Ancient Taoist teaching recommends abstaining from alcohol, meat, beans, and grains. There are many more additional teachings as we've discovered in a previous chapter. Balance in diet is key though within Taoism.

The Essence of Taoism

In essence, Taoism emphasizes the harmony of the human being with nature. The teaching of Taoism is attached to the Chinese culture. Therefore, it's very difficult to separate this teaching from daily life, especially if you're from a Chinese heritage.

Taoism existed before the time of Confucius. Taoism is also often called Tao. According to most followers, Tao is the main force within the universe that's found in all things, and it's the core of all things in heaven, and upon the earth. These are said to be both eternal and immutable.

The Sectioning of Taoist Teachings

Generally speaking, the development of Taoist teachings can be sectioned into the relationship of human beings to the universe, the relationship of human beings to God, the relationship of human beings to peers, and also the relationship of human beings to their own personal life. All teachings cover all aspects of life.

In fact, the *Tao Te Ching* is the best place to start. Did you know that the *Tao Te Ching* is the smallest holy book amongst all the various religions in the world? Actually, *Tao Te Ching* consists of only 81 short poems and is a mere 25 pages long.

Sometimes it's difficult for ordinary people to understand the contents of the book because it's very poetic. In addition to the *Tao Te Ching*, there are many other texts that are considered by experts as key Taoist philosophies, and are mentioned within this title within the *Suggested Reading* list.

Taoism in Culture

Taoism in the development of Chinese society had an extraordinary impact on culture. And one of the most influential teachings is by Lao Tzu. Lao Tzu's teachings can be developed and allowed for within various aspects of community life, including religious practices, philosophical knowledgeability, health, well-being, and a general understanding of life, including nature and peer relationships with the self and with others.

Taoism brings calm and peace so that people regain the happiness that might have been lost due to oppression and war in ancient times. Taoist teachings are still ongoing and developing today, even in modern times. This expansion is part of the essence of Tao.

The Spirit of Taoism

Now, the spirit of Taoism can be found in a love of spiritual calm and the soul's intrinsic need for peace. Some find this within wisdom, or tranquility, in well-being, through charity, in growth, and in preserving life and supporting nature. The spirit of Taoism is within poetry, song, dance, drawing, and painting, and the beauty of nature, or the calmness of practicing yoga or laughing with a friend. This Taoist purposefulness leads Chinese society to a wonderment, a calmness, a humble pride, a trueness of simplicity, and the freedom from mere desire for desire's sake.

Additionally, living in harmony with nature has brought the lives of Chinese people much peace and calm. This is the influence of the soul of life becoming united with nature. And here, with the inclusion of Lao Tzu's teachings in Chinese civilization, this formed a society that was simple, but not overly primitive. In fact, they rejected the instruments of war, luxury, and greediness, and opted for a simpler, more balanced way of living.

The most wonderful part is that Taoism teaches humans about the peacefulness of life. This comes from the heart and soul and is a necessary part of Taoist belief. Additionally, nature supports us to achieve that peace. To truly be at peace with nature and our own selves is key. And this is so we'll more easily carry out our daily activities, doing so without the burden of negative (or useless) thoughts.

Taoism as a Teacher

Taoism also teaches many things about the life sciences, including Eastern medicine, meditation, breathing (as a science), philosophy, and martial arts, too. This knowledge is excellent for daily activities and living with ease.

There is no actual Taoist philosophical routine. In fact, since philosophical Taoism has never been formalized into a true curriculum, religious Taoists have many different routines which are followed, with each corresponding with a time of year, time of day, and what they're trying to achieve.

Mostly during the morning, it's normal in Quanzhen Taoism to recite several scriptures which may include:

1. The quiet and clarity classic

2. The Yellow Emperor subtle inscription of the heart classic

3. The classic of listening for Tai Shang's echo

In a modern capacity, meditation, Qigong, and martial arts masters came up with different ideas about when to practice. Some individuals believe it's better to practice in the early morning and late at night, where meditation is concerned. Usually though, night-time practices take place between 11 pm to 1 am, and this is to match up with the water cycle of the moon.

In the morning, some people like to practice directly after waking up, so that they may soothe the mind and heart into being functional for the day. Others prefer to meditate between 11 am to 1 pm because it matches up with the fire element and the noon sun time.

Usually though, individuals will mediate more often around the winter solstice and in the time around the highest moon of the month. There's also a saying that says, "Meditating at the solstice is worth half a year of practice."

Some Other Key Elements to Know

- Knowing the Germs
- Power, will, and ambition in life
- Daily I-Ching
- Non-doing and going with the flow
- Emptiness (wu), and the benefit of emptying your mind
-

Delving Deeper into Taoism & the Science Quest

For many practicing Taoists, the relationship between Taoism and modern biological science is too technical and esoteric. Many individuals might be more than curious as to how

Taoism relates to real, crucial science, and this is so because science is the underpinning of so much of our modern life in general.

Many Taoist habits fit nicely into life, and you might even believe that Taoism and science aren't truly complementary, especially because of their very different origins. And you'd be right to believe this, however, Taoism and science have a lot in common, and quite amazingly so. But yes, there are differences too.

Let's speak firstly of Tao. In Taoism, Tao is known as the truest pattern of existence, or the path that's revealed in the existence between matter and energy. Tao agrees with the inherent property of each phenomenon within the cosmos, in fact. Okakura speaks of the Tao as "the mood of the universe" in his book *The Book of Tea*. Tao is also the process generating the patterns that we can see, including the dynamic of generating "things as they are."

The Tao is therefore characterized by order, by patterning, and by harmony as prerequisites. Tao of the cosmos allows for the evolution of life and is also supportive of life, even though life is said to be nothing special, and just seen as another aspect of the unfolding of Tao.

In truth, the scientific enterprise of the West of the last 200 hundred years is that: reality truly has an order and a patterning to it. The scientific equivalent is the discovery of the order within the universe, and the description of that order in actual mathematical models which can be truly studied. When a mathematical description is truly precise, the relationships are known as "laws."

It's also important to note that physics and chemistry have succeeded in discovering many true laws. And when the relationships being described are too overwhelming for precise mathematical description, the relationships are called "theories." The field of biology has discovered many interesting theories, and these are explanations that have been subjected to scientific tests without being contradicted. The test models for explanations have been utilized over and over again.

Additionally, science has also found that the properties of matter are inherent to matter. So, the 'nature' of reality incorporates that of reality's physical properties, rather than being imposed from outside of the system. Also, matter and energy are linked and can transform back and forth as described via the *Laws of Thermodynamics*. Interestingly too, science has discovered that life is founded on the same laws and properties as inanimate reality, and this is huge news for many science enthusiasts. At the deepest level, life actually emerges from the exact physical properties and interactions amongst atoms and molecules that characterize natural elements like water, rocks, and fire, as examples.

Ultimately, there is no, one unified theory or formulation of all of reality, by way of mathematical or descriptive terms, per say. The concept of Tao might be considered an informal summary of the overarching pattern of order, however, and the process of transformation discovered by the realm of the science field. Actually, Tao is quite consistent with what science has discovered about order, patterning, inherent properties, transformative processes related to energy, and the most common properties of life, including various forms of non-living phenomena.

The Importance of Qi

The energetic medium where the transformative flow of the Tao is expressed is known as Qi. The Chinese word "Qi" can be translated to "energy," but it has far richer implications because it relates to also meaning breath, air, steam, force, strength, and temper as well. This perfectly exudes the manifestation or flow of Tao, firstly turning this way, then that, and endlessly transforming and moving. By choosing to express the flow of Tao in terms of energy, Taoism truly emphasizes the symbiotic vitality of nature's pulsing and flow.

Yin & Yang Principles as Energy States

Yin includes all the energetic states that incorporate the yielding, passive, shady, lunar, earthly, and more feminine aspects of life, and yang exudes the aggressive, dominant, bright, solar, heavenly, and more masculine aspects of life. Most importantly, these two poignant factors are in the flow of Qi and are not opposites, but complementary, in fact.

Each reality is composed of aggregate combinations of yin and yang in their own unique and truly balanced incorporations. It's the interplay of these composures that are well characterized by constant transformation of yin elements to yang, and vice versa. Additionally, the Qi flows, and so transformation becomes the normality. Those who are wise in the ways of the flow of Qi claim to discern the paths of flow in mountains and rivers, and within the human body too. Traditional Chinese medicine and acupuncture relies heavily upon the knowledge of Qi pathways in humans to rectify blockages and/or inconsistencies within the harmonious flow of Qi.

We can see that in science there's a similar emphasis on energetics. The great findings of the *Laws of Thermodynamics* explain to us that matter and energy are the two grand states of reality, and that each is progressively transforming into the other (known as *The First Law*). The true quantitative parameters of the universal matter-energy interchange have been solved, reflecting modern science's emphasis on mathematical formulation and its importance. And so, this energy, like Qi's definitions, can exist in various forms, each capable of transforming into the other. Among these states are what are known as potential energy, kinetic energy, chemical energy, and nuclear energy.

The Second Law from the *Laws of Thermodynamics* describes how developed systems (such as living creatures) need a constant input of energy to maintain their structure. This is due to the universal tendency for organization to decay and is known as "entropy." Studies within the field of biology have found that the in-flow of energy is critical to organisms as well as their ecosystems, and have been able to quantify the parameters of this flow into life, as well as through the multiple ecological layers within life.

The important news here is that: life exists on the earth only because of energy-yielding phenomenon which enter the earth's thin band of life at two known places. Chemical energy enters at fissures within the oceans' floors, as energy-rich streams of lava. These steam up and spew and are coming from the molten center of the planet. It's also known that enormous mats of bacteria have developed around these fissures, and ancient creatures which can extract energy from this heat source can (and do) support their own lives. Extremely monumental communities have developed around these hectares of bacterial mats too, which are deep atop the ocean's floor, feeding on the bacteria in level after level of energy transformation. In addition, other pockets of chemical energy are harvested by other ancient creatures known as the Archaeans. They exist scattered closer to the surface of the planet in the extreme environments favored by them, like hot springs and highly saline sources of water.

The second true in-flow of energy supporting life on the planet is the sun, Earth's very own star. The solar energy pours to the earth, and some creatures from various domains and kingdoms of life have developed the innate ability to utilize solar radiation and convert it to life-supporting aid. In fact, the process of photosynthesis is one such example that's truly noteworthy.

The amazing photosynthetic capture of solar energy is widespread over the entire surface of our earth (both marine life and terrestrial life), with levels of transformation of this biological energy flowing through the upper levels to include carnivores, herbivores, and the decomposers of these important ecosystems.

Qi is therefore considered to be an informal summary of the various energetic flows and transformations mapped out quantitatively and exactly by the modern science field. Like Tao, the term "Qi" cannot be admitted into any one faction of science, but can stand as a surprisingly true formulation that includes many of the general features of energy flow as already discovered within the sciences.

Human beings are most interested in their own place on the earth. In the Taoist viewpoint, however, human beings are said to be nothing extraordinary, but simply one of the "ten thousand creatures." We have our own unique traits, being primarily the complexity of our central nervous system, and our resulting hyper-sensitivity to Qi, both in and around us.

Each individual creature has its own unique characteristics. Additionally, the Taoist refusal to place humans on a pedestal is made with clarity throughout the Taoist sources of writings and is also found within the ancient and modern Taoist approaches to life.

The Chang Tzu

"Everything has its own nature and its own function," says the *Chuang Tzu*. "Nothing is without nature or function. Consider a small stalk or a great column, a leper or a beauty, things that are great or wicked, perverse, or strong. They are all one in Tao."

The Chuang Tzu asks these poignant questions:

"If a man sleeps in a damp place, his back will ache, and he will be half-paralyzed. But does this happen to eels?"

"If a man lives up in tree, he will tremble with fright. But does this happen to monkeys? Of these three, who knows the right place to live?"

"Mao Chiang and Li Chi are considered beautiful by men. But if fish saw them, they would dive to the bottom of the river. If birds saw them, they would fly off. If deer saw them, they would run away. Of these four, who recognizes real beauty?"

It's interesting to note that Western science began as a Christian, religious corporation, and within it the description of God's creation. But as the descriptions of the world grew more pronounced, it became apparent that the creation differed in many respects from its formulation within the Christian religion. This is just a comparison with Taoism for comparison's sake.

In the first instance, the earth was discovered *not* to be the center of the solar system, or even the universe. Then, humans were discovered not to be fundamentally different than the rest of creation, either. Other creatures can also think, dream, sing, utilize language, create, use tools, and even pay homage to their dead, scientists have learned. Human beings didn't emerge from a distinct creation event, but instead evolved from other apes, according to one viewpoint, following the same rules in the same manner as every other plant and animal species which has since evolved from its bloodline of ancestors.

The blood in humans' veins is salty because our distant relatives of old originated in the same primeval oceans as every other descendant of those ancestors. Our DNA even uses the same nucleotides and the same genetic code as bacteria, banana slugs, redwood, and every other creature on the earth, in fact. These truths about the scientific view of the place of humans in the natural world is completely consistent with the Taoist perspective, it seems. Additionally, many of the fundamental ideas of Tao, Qi, and the place of humans are all incredibly similar in both Taoism and science. This is not the case with Christianity, our comparative religion, however.

The Similarity of Reversion

According to Taoists, the world works in certain cycles with things returning (or reverting) sooner or later to the beginning point. "The ten thousand things rise and fall while the self watches their return," says the *Tao Te Ching*. And, "They grow and flourish and then return to the source. Returning to the source is the way of stillness, which is the way of nature." Lao Tzu also stated that "Returning is the motion of the Tao."

Ecologists have found that the elements present on the earth pass through a cyclic system of movements. Nitrogen passes from the soil to plants, from plants to animals and then via decay, back to the soil in a systematic cycle. Here, two linked cyclical processes occur, and because the element may flow from the atmosphere to the soil, and then back to the atmosphere from the soil. And this is completely due to the action of microorganisms. A marvelous infrastructure, indeed.

The "nitrogen cycle" works relatively smoothly and functions by means of the activity via the host of living creatures. This occurs from bacteria to carnivores and through organic chemical processes.

Ancient Taoists were understanding of certain aspects of this nitrogen cycle, which is disclosed in *Tao Te Ching*: "When the Tao is present in the Universe, the horses haul manure." Speaking here about how human beings are actually participating in the grand cycling movement.

Complementary Aspects

Taoists mostly view reality as being composed of processes and phenomena that can generally be categorized into two great understandings, namely being yin and yang. The major point is that yin and yang are not opposed to each other. And, as we know, yin and yang are complementary, being that they balance each other out in a symbiotic wonderment which is shown throughout existence and throughout the entire universe. We can see; they're both necessary components of the whole, as illustrated in the well-known yin yang symbology of two, conjoining, curved shapes. This outlook contrasts with the standard Western outlook, which sees the contrast of opposites as being otherworldly or different, and antagonistic to the other. Think of the common views of good versus evil, male versus female, right versus wrong, love versus hate, black versus white. These are prevalent in modern society today.

Scientific Explanation

The natural processes of biology can 'see' two interacting systems, which frequently possess similarities to the yin yang modeling. One example is the sympathetic and parasympathetic components of the autonomic nervous system, which is thoroughly studied by physiologists who work with these systems.

Ecology experts speak of the evolution of organisms being governed by either r-selection or by k-selection. Selection pressures can change, and a k-selected species might transform to an r-selected form, just as Taoists see yin and yang constantly transforming into the other. It's truly mind-blowing when you discover some of these influences within science and throughout Taoism.

Other scientists have found that the human cerebrum functions as two interconnected halves. The left half works in sequences of analytical thought processes, including language, and time processing (yang properties). The right half specializes in the intuitive thought processes, including aspects of art, music, and spatial processing (yin properties).

Scientists realize too, that there's an evidential need to adopt the yin yang viewpoint, where various explanations are viewed as being not as opposed and exclusive, but instead, as being complementary to the other. An example might be that of long-distance navigation taken on by migrating birds.

The End of Life as a Process

Taoists view passing away as an integral part of the natural process, but not as an unnatural event or an enemy of one's life.

World-famous Lao Tzu speaks to a cripple who has just been rebuffed by Confucius, He stated "Why don't you simply make him (Confucius) see that life and death are one thread, the same line viewed from different sides--and thus free him from his cuffs and fetters."

Science views death as an essential part of the process of organic change that also includes life. Without death, new life and new life formations simply can't occur.

In truth, the view of the role of death in natural processes affects the view of human death. The Taoists refused to see death as a misfortune, however, or even to fear death. Death was simply another transformational process, and transformation is truly part of Tao.

Some Taoist texts indicate plainly that they were not entirely sure what happened after death, but they certainly were not going to fear it.

"How can I tell if love of life is not a delusion," from the *Chuang Tzu*. "How can I tell whether a man who fears death is not like a man who has left home and dreads returning? Lady Li was the daughter of a border guard of Ai. When the Duke of Chin first took her captive, she wept until her dress was soaked with tears. But once she was living in the Duke's palace, sharing his bed, and eating delicious food, she wondered why she had ever cried. How can I tell whether the dead are not amazed that they ever clung to life?"

And so, since ancient times, Taoists seem to accept death as the end of one's existence as a personality upon the earth. And it's this perception invoking calm and acceptance of the cessation of life, and it's not solidified with the need for an afterlife, like in other religious traditions, per say.

"The true man of old knew nothing about loving life or hating death," is stated from the *Chuang Tzu*. "When he was born, he felt no elation. When he entered death, there was no sorrow. Carefree he went. Carefree he came. That was all. . . He accepted what was given with delight, and when it was gone, he gave it no more thought."

Notable Similarities Within Western Science & Taoism

Some notable similarities occur between modern Western science and the ancient Chinese perception throughout Taoism. The *Tao Te Ching* asked "How do I know the universe is like this?" It clarified it immediately, stating "By looking!"

We might see the basis of the similarities, including the methods employed by each, and that they are the same. Modern science bases knowledge on careful observation of the natural world. Even in the experimental method, observing a situation in which only one variable has changed. And so, we see that Taoists also arrive at their outlook on the universe by intrinsically observing it, and by looking at it with a clear, unclouded mindset.

"There is nothing like using restraint. Restraint begins with giving up one's own ideas," says the *Tao Te Ching*.

Observing the Ancient Taoists

The Taoists of traditional China were located throughout the woods and mountains, and the central gardens and parklands, too. They spent a vast amount of time sitting nearby streams or wandering through forests in contentment.

Many Chinese landscape paintings have captured them over many centuries of superb artworks, quietly and attentively observing streams from a small hut, or walking amidst groves of trees, or perhaps bamboo. And always in nature and observing its features. And because these Taoists knew the natural world so intimately, there were many nature metaphors and examples within texts like the *Tao Te Ching* and the *Chuang Tzu*.

"A man is born gentle and weak. At his death he is hard and stiff. Green plants are tender and filled with sap. At their death they are withered and dry." - *Tao Te Ching*

"Chuang Tzu replied, 'Have you ever watched a wildcat or a weasel? It crouches close to the ground and waits for its prey.

Then it leaps up and down, first one way, then the other, until it catches and kills its prey.'" - *Chuang Tzu*

"Do you know the story of the praying mantis? . . . Do you know how a tiger trainer works? He knows when the tigers are hungry and when they are full. Thereby he is in touch with their fierce nature." - *Chuang Tzu*

It's clear that Taoism and science have a common way of gathering information to build a particularly logical view of reality, and so they also share a common sentient-type-source of knowledge. In cases of contrasting viewpoints though, the deciding judgment comes not from a book, or from an individual's judgment. More logically, the final decider is the phenomenon itself. The scientist might go back to the field, or back to the lab, and looks at the phenomenon again, using a new technique or experiment to find answers. The Taoist goes back to the natural world and calmly and patiently watches the flow of the way nature unfolds, including the steady progression of seasonal changes or influences. Reality can be carefully observed and is the source of knowledge and the final decider in both Taoism and within science.

Fundamental Differences Are Notable When Comparing Taoism & Science

It's important to note, however, that even through the fundamental similarities between Taoism and science, there are also some obvious differences to see. Some of these ways in which the two differ are important.

Argumentativeness

Taoists dislike argument and lack trust in people with verbal egoic traits, in fact.

"Those who know do not talk. Those who talk do not know," is expressed in *Tao Te Ching*. "Truthful words are not beautiful. Beautiful words are not truthful. Good men do not argue. Those who argue are not good."

Scientists, comparatively, enjoy the spirited exchange of opinions and argument/debate, either verbally or within text. They use the peer review system to judge requests for grants where articles for publication are concerned. Criticism is rife, and many scientists simply agree to disagree with one another.

Machine Usage

Taoists have deep suspicions about those who use machines. The *Tao Te Ching* describes the ideal country as follows. "A small country has fewer people. Though there are machines that can work ten to a hundred times faster than man, they are not needed. . . Though there are boats and carriages, no one uses them. . . Men return to the knotting of rope in place of writing."

It's important to note, that this aversion to machines is not occurring in science, where machines are seen as facets to expand the range of observations. Additionally, it's impossible to do modern science independent of the array of microscopes and the myriad of other instruments and equipment which have opened up worlds of observation and modes of quantification. In fact, the world of science would virtually be closed without these machines and tools. To a large degree, the history of modern science is the story of the invention of the machines used within its investigations, and throughout the different fields of science.

Experimentation

Another significant difference is within the area of experimentation. Although objective observation is the pivotal necessity of science, the most powerful use of this act is when the observation of one situation is compared to another situation, being identical to the first except, in one angle, whereby the experimental (or independent) variable is changed. By manipulation, the phenomenon under observation is inclusive of the effect of the variable.

In Taoism, there's no such thing as an experimental method, much less an expressed understanding of its need within the discovery and description of any natural processes. Also, there's an unmistakable sense of distaste for human manipulation of the natural world within the realm of Taoism, in fact.

Embracing the All

"Do you think you can take over the universe and improve it? I do not believe it can be done. The universe is sacred. You cannot improve it. If you try to change it, you will ruin it. If you try to hold it, you will lose it" - *Tao Te Ching*

Taoists are not striving to mentally process the efforts of evil only, but they see manipulative human beings trying to change and control the world for their own selfish gain and greed. The humble, sincere, honest, and good efforts of humans to improve the world are just as distasteful to Taoists, however. In the Taoist way of viewing reality, the world is perfect just as it is. Any attempt to force it into some other configuration inevitably unbalances it, regardless of the motive. Accept it all. Embrace it all. This is said to be true wisdom.

Consistencies in Perspective

It's true that the fundamental similarities we have noted between Taoism and modern science are just that, they are merely similarities, and not identities or adherents. This text is not trying to dictate anything regarding science or Taoism but is merely observing the similarities and differences here.

It is true though, that in ancient times, Taoists knew that cycles were common and important within the scope of natural systems. They didn't know that the element nitrogen occurs in the atmosphere, or that it's fixed into nitrate by microorganisms that live in the soil, or that plants take it up in this form and mix it with hydrogen and carbon atoms to form protein molecules. Science really just takes Taoism and allows it to be proven, with a factual, measurable, provable, logical methodology.

Taoism, quite interestingly, has known from early history that that humans possess two aspects to their personalities, one being assertive, rational, and verbal, and the other being receptive, intuitive, and nonverbal. They didn't truly know that the former set of characteristics are primarily processed by the left cerebral hemisphere, and the other characteristics by the right. They also didn't realize that the brain is composed of millions of neurons which communicate with each other by means of chemicals crossing over via the gaps between the cells.

Taoists did notice that certain life forms on the earth were endlessly transforming and had arisen from a common origin of ancestry. They didn't know that differential reproductive fitness from natural selection powered these changes of evolution, nor did they ask whether or not the changes occurred by the gradual accumulation of minor changes, or by swifter, major changes.

Even with the differences in time, culture, motivation, and outlook, the particularness of essential similarities between the ancient viewpoint of Taoism and the modern scientific enterprise is seen. This agreeability argues strongly for a fundamental continuity of mental processes within the human mind, as well as for a fundamental forward process in the structure of reality. The ancient Taoists, lacking an appreciation for mathematics and the systematic use of experiments, except within their study of alchemy, did come a surprisingly long way toward certain fundamental acknowledgements of modern science. And, essentially by adhering to the cornerstone of that science. With these being careful, considerate, and objective observation of the natural world around them.

This is well noted by an English biochemist, sinologist, and a man who was a historian of science, namely Joseph Needham, who showed by careful study that stated how Taoism was the fertile ground out of which early science arose in China, and which moved early science in the West for the first 14 centuries A.D.

In 1956 Needham wrote *Science and Civilization in China* and later, his 1981 summary called *Science and Traditional China*. These titles will be added to the *Suggested Reading* list found at the end of this title.

The true brilliance of it all is how far the ancient Taoists *did* come, and merely by observation, including their sharp, informed intuition proceeding out of that which they observed. When generations someday take a look back on modern science today, they will perhaps wonder at our ignorance and the incompleteness of what we thought we knew before.

The early Taoists saw so much by simply observing it, and without machines they gained so much amazing knowledge, all sustained through humility and by keeping their eyes on the cyclical occurrences and processes within nature. A truly astounding feat, really.

Chapter 8: Putting Taoism into Practice in Your Daily Life

The Taoist tradition has given rise to a 'mountain' of everyday habits of the ordinary people of China, and these habits which contribute to a rich, humbler experience of life. These everyday Taoist habits work just as well for modern followers as the Chinese, though.

Trying to find the calm, peace and serenity is a great way to start. Balance too, is key. A work-life balance and finding oneself to be still even in the seeming chaos of modern-day life.

We've all witnessed such scenes. Maybe you're the one doing the running or the walking. Why do these particular activities make us feel so good? Why do people carve time out of their busy days to walk, to run, or to visit a park by themselves or with their friends and family?

At the Heart of China is Nature

The same sort of scenes occur even now, throughout the heart of China, in fact, although the details might be a little different. There, you can see crowds of people doing the beautiful, sweeping moves of Tai Chi, or the violent lunges of Kung Fu with swords and lances being utilized. Some might simply be walking deliberately along a route or course, with their hands describing their conversations in circular movements in the air.

When you survey Chinese art, you might notice how many paintings there are of lone individuals or small groups of people in the mountains, or in a bamboo grove, or maybe beside a stream. This was mentioned a little earlier, and it's important to note once again. Usually these people are playing a friendly board game, or enjoying tea, or sometimes just sitting quietly, peacefully enjoying the scenery or natural setting.

What's occurring in these traditional activities? Are the Chinese participating in the same sort of experience as Westerners might do? In China, people do these outdoor activities because the Taoist outlook permeating Chinese culture places a huge importance on humans connecting with the forces inherent within the natural world, a world where nature is key. This keeps people both healthy *and* happy. And the natural world is truly Tao. These people, therefore, are connecting with Tao. Could it truly be that simple? Perhaps, yes.

The Tao Consists of Flow

Tao confers the inherent nature of each material and force within the cosmos. Tao is the background and the gumption for everything that happens, in a flow with myriads of processes of transformation that constantly course through the world in which we live. In the words of a Japanese scholar, Tao is said to be, "...the mood of the universe." The flow of Tao gives enablement to the patterns and regularities that characterize the universe. Tao courses everywhere, but most clearly in the natural world around us, where its patterns are strikingly evident, desperately cyclical, and most accessible to human perception and our participation within it.

So, human beings connect with this most elemental of phenomena by spending time in nature, and by participating in the flow of life within nature. Activities in nature remind us of the way things are and might even realign us with the mood of the universe, the core of existence, including our own existence, as well as everything else within the cosmos.

A major key to Taoism is simply to spend time in the natural world. And immersing ourselves in Tao is the most basic of Taoist habits. This is so crucial to our health, including our mental, physical and spiritual needs, that it should be done on a daily basis to really be felt.

But how do we daily immerse ourselves in the Tao in the West?

Disallowing or quitting your job and family priorities and moving to a shack in the woods is not necessarily required, but some do take this route of living.

Do you have a park or a natural space reasonably close to your home? Go there, every day, if possible. Make it a guaranteed and routine part of your day. If you're an early person, then early morning is prime time. We all know the air is fresher, with the day more charged with positive potential just after dawn. This is a spiritual observation, and many other religions note this, too. A prime time to be out in the natural world.

If you're not an early morning person, then visit the park on your lunch hour, or first thing after studying or after work. In general, engaging in some type of movement among the trees and rocks is best. You might try walking, running, cycling. But just sitting in the natural environment is beneficial too, especially near a water source, in fact.

Sometimes, just warming yourself in the sunshine can do wonders. Doing this and breathing in the fresh air is a great way to feel good. And there are loads of studies which support the need for Vitamin D as a crucial part of health and well-being.

If you're not close to a park or you're not particularly athletic at all, don't worry. If you have a bit of dirt around your home, start a vegetable or flower garden. Tend to it as much of the year as your climate within your locality permits. You could mulch it, fertilize it, take deep breaths as you work with the soil, drawing into your lungs the delicious dirt smell produced by the millions of bacteria residing there. Don't do this with garden potting mixes though, there are warnings on these bags from your garden center.

You could even start a compost pile if your neighbors don't mind, and maybe recycle your food and lawn waste. Chickens are great if you have room for them, and they can eat the scraps from your cooking waste. Tending to your own garden puts you in touch with the flow of Tao, focusing you on the natural rhythms of the universe. And the beauty of it is that it's only as far away as your own backyard.

Immersion in Tao Through Nature

Some keen ideas for you:

Walk or jog in a park
Notice the trees and rocks
Eat lunch outside
Take note of clouds and breezes
Sit near a lake, creek, or by the ocean
Take time to explore rocks and creatures
Cycle in the countryside
Take a picnic, pick some flowers
Start a small garden
Feel the dirt, make it richer

If you don't have a park or any usable dirt nearby, you could bring the natural world into your own home. Invest in some different types of house plants, and care for them with passion. Learn which of your windows the plants are happiest beside. Which water schedules they thrive on, too. Which nutrients keep them healthy and greenest. Do they need extra light in the wintertime to stay happy? Tao flows in electrical appliances, too. Energy is everywhere, in fact, and electricity is included here. There is no right or wrong, just flow.

So, what natural object intrigues you when you go for a vacation or a walk? You can pick it up, bring it home, and put it on your windowsill. You might like to find rocks and seashells and place them on shelves and counters, as well as windowsills. Not just any rocks or seashells, but special ones that you truly admire. Like colorful seashells, or seashells formed by mollusks that have poison darts to subdue their prey. Just seeing the rocks and shells there, might remind you of how incredible the world is, and how much fun you had when you found them. If you like, you could buy jewelery with crystals or elements of nature within them. The most fun part is using your imagination, in fact.

Exploring Terrain

Visit every park or green space in your locality over the next week or month. Describe each one, and the possibilities each one offers for the immersion in Tao. You might also like to visit every source of water in your region over the next month or year. Describe each one as best you can, and the possibilities each one offers for immersion in Tao.

Learn to identify some of the native trees in your region. Describe their leaf shape, what type of fruit they produce, if any, and what types of birds and insects or mammals you find near them (or in them).

You can purchase binoculars and learn about some of the common birds in your area. What vegetation to they enjoy the most, and why? What do they like to eat? What do their bird calls sound like? You could take photos or even videos of them in their habitat.

Work & Home-Friendly Ideas

If you work in a space where there's no nature, you could have lunch outside the office, just to get some sunshine or perhaps see what color the sky is that particular day. If this isn't possible, you can find a guided meditation on the YouTube platform and listen to nature sounds, like the ocean, a breeze, or perhaps even a waterfall.

You can open your windows as much as possible. Don't hide inside your closed home or office with a heater or air conditioner on. In the summer, at night, you might like to open your windows, and let nature cool the house or office space down if you work from home.

Camping to Get Closer to Nature

Do you ever go camping? You might like to include camping trips into your family or social life. A large family tent is great if you have children or friends who don't mind sleeping close by. It can be a part of your essential vacation or down time, where you use it to enjoy each other's company while you discover the wonderment of nature.

Make it fun. How many matches do you need to start the fire? You could use newspapers as kindling. At what age might your kids get better at making the fire than the parents? Which trail are you all hiking today? Who will cook?

If You Have Children - Camping Fun

You can buy "light sticks," which are those plastic tubes containing substances which glow when you break the internal partition separating them and take them camping with you. You can entertain yourselves for hours after settling into bedrolls in the tent, swirling the glowing containers in different patterns on the end of a string, or bending the long, more flexible ones into cool, fun shapes. For kids, they can try their hand at making butterflies which flutter around the tent, or lumbering big bears, or other animal shapes they love. The kids can nestle beside the glowing sticks, their own personal guardians throughout the night.

Sit and Plan a Camping Trip with Family or Friends

Your Ideas:
Possible sites within two hours from home:
Unusual food treats to bring:
For simple entertainment... light sticks and:
Fire-making necessities:
Field guides for hikes, animal sightings:
One comfort from home:
Something weird to bring:
Tent, raingear, torches, other essentials:
Food:
Clothing:
Clock, compass and:

The Natural World is Who We Are

Human beings evolved for millions of years on the savannas of Africa. They eventually moved out of Africa and into the rest of what is known as the "Old World," then to the "New World," living freely, and being completely immersed in nature.

It's true too, that sensory input from the natural world is also part of our biological heritage, and part of what has been incorporated into the normal functioning of our genetics, our nervous systems, and our DNA. When we cut ourselves off from the natural world, our biological systems are lost, missing key elements of the system of cues they are accustomed to receive, historically speaking.

Sensory input from the natural world is so fundamental that, like sea creatures in water, we don't even realize how critical it is. But just look at people living in crowded cities. Many of them feel disconnected, off-track, or feel frazzled and off-center, with some wondering what's gone wrong, or what's missing from their lives.

A Last Expression in Nature

Tiny frogs inhabit rainforests in the heart of South America. These are the creatures which produce the deadly alkaloid poisons that Cocos Indians rub on their darts to bring down larger prey when they're hunting, actually.

Interestingly, the alkaloids in the atmosphere cause sodium and potassium channels within the cell membranes to malfunction. When you capture a Dendrobatid frog and take it to a laboratory in a city, the amphibian ceases producing the poisons that usually protect it. *But why?* We still can't figure it out, even with the help of science. At first the food was questioned. *But was it the food source/s?* No.

There's truly something wonderful about living in that rainforest environment which turns on the frog's poisonous genes to express themselves within that environment. Perhaps it's the sounds. Or maybe it's the smells. It might be the whole experience of living in the natural world where it evolved. But remove it from those inputs, and it's missing something. It's just not quite right, as if a piece is missing from it. And in this case, that piece is quite literal.

People are like frogs. We all evolved in the natural, physical world. We need it, to stay healthy, for our well-being, to alleviate stress, and to keep our systems functioning well, overall.

When individuals are taken out of the natural environment they were meant to live in, isolating them from the natural world and its flow of Tao, it is then that humans can really suffer.

Immerse yourself in Tao. It keeps you centered, happier, healthier, and it promotes longevity, too. It can enable us to be more resilient as well. The Tao is the sacred flow of the cosmos, the heart of nature, including its processes, and its cyclical ways of being.

Finding Your Place of Beingness

Truly finding your own place of stillness or beingness is a blessed part of Taoism. An outdoor space that just makes you feel good to be there is key. A spot that makes you feel connected to the cosmos can work wonders. A wonderful location where Tao fits with your own nature, and makes you want to stay there for longer.

You may find your place at one of the parks in your region, or maybe near a babbling brook or in a picturesque setting within your own backyard. Or you may want to drive out to the countryside, close by to the mountains, or to the seashore to find it. But you'll know it when you do. There'll be a rightness to its look and feel. A sigh of contentment and joy will be there for you, and you'll feel at peace and calmer while you're there. But whatever place it is, let it be *your* sanctuary, a place where you feel as though you connect to you, to nature, and to Tao. And what a wonderful place it will be.

References:

Asia Times, Francesco Sisci, Asia Editor of La Stampa, September 2, 2010

Birgitta Augustin Institute of Fine Arts, New York University, Metropolitan Museum of Art metmuseum.org

Christine Gross-Loh, The Atlantic, October 8, 2013

Chow Chung-yan, South China Morning Post, December 30, 2012

Ian Johnson, New York Review of Books, November 10, 2011

Ian Johnson, NY Review of Books, January 13, 2012

Robert Eno, Indiana University indiana.edu

Stanford Encyclopedia of Philosophy, December 17, 2014

Suggested Reading:

Chang Tzu

Book of Songs

Holy Bible

Holy Quran

I Ching

Myth and Meaning in Early Taoism: The Theme of Chaos (hun-tun) - N.J. Myth

Science and Civilization in China - Joseph Needham

Science and Traditional China - Joseph Needham

Taoist Long-Life Diet - Lee Style

Tao Te Ching - Lao Tzu

The Book of Tea - Okakura

The Complete System of Self-Healing: Internal Exercises - Dr. Stephen Chang

The Great Tao - Dr. Stephen Chang

The Taoist Art of K'ai Men - Chee Soo

The Tao of Balanced Diet: Secrets of a Thin & Healthy Body - Dr. Stephen Chang

The Tao of Sexology: The Book of Infinite Wisdom - Dr. Stephen Chang

www.ingramcontent.com/pod-product-compliance
Lightning Source LLC
Chambersburg PA
CBHW071417070526
44578CB00003B/590